D1525184

TURNER PUBLISHING

PADUCAH, KENTUCKY

TURNER PUBLISHING COMPANY
412 Broadway, P.O. Box 3101
Paducah, KY 42002-3101
270-443-0121

Turner Publishing Company Staff:
Keith R. Steele, Publishing Consultant
Charlotte Harris, Project Coordinator
Peter Zuniga, Designer

Library of Congress Control Number: 2001088338
ISBN: 1-56311-718-5

Limited Edition. Printed in the U.S.A.

Page one: Statue honoring police work. Located outside Philadelphia Police Dept. Headquarters. Photograph property of Efraim Nathan.

TABLE OF CONTENTS

DEDICATION

For all the fallen,

all the partners,

all the widows,

and all the children.

ACKNOWLEDGMENTS

I would like to begin by thanking David and Gloria Basner, Catherine Maverick Schoetz, Patricia B. McRae, Karen Thompson, Kim Phillips, D. Vance Brewington, Brian Cordeiro, David L. Beckmann, Sara Cohen, Sarah Friedman, Heather "Ariel" Lintz, Lower Merion Township, Pennsylvania Police Officer Jane M. Tucker, and Concerns of Police Survivors Executive Director Suzie Sawyer. All of these good people selflessly made themselves available to read, and comment on, the original manuscript. Their time and suggestions are much appreciated.

A special acknowledgment goes to Nick Feliciani who provided me with an essential piece of research information that would otherwise have been unavailable. I thank him for his assistance.

I owe a hearty "thank you" to Kurt Slafkovsky, For a Tin Star's one-man publicity machine. Kurt, I cannot wait to shake your hand.

My appreciation for all the photography work are due to Jim MacMillan, Michael Mercanti, the *Philadelphia Daily News*, the *New York Times*, Kelly Houston, Jedediah Baker, David M. Basner, Efraim Nathan, and Catherine Schoetz.

Thanks go to Zachary Ross Mannheimer, for his continuous support, respect, and faith in my writing.

I must also take my hat off to Bobbi Wolf, a woman who has taught me many things, perhaps most importantly that having a cause is just as important as having a heart.

Next, I would like to extend my gratitude to the Chairman of the National Law Enforcement Officers Memorial,

Craig Floyd. Not only did Chairman Floyd appreciate and encourage me in my endeavors concerning this book, but he also directed me to Turner Publishing, so I also thank him for that, as well as all of the wonderful work he does at the Memorial.

In that same breath, a tremendous standing ovation goes to Keith Steele, Dave Turner, Charlotte Harris, Peter Zuniga, and everybody at Turner Publishing who worked to make this a reality.

"Part of this book also goes to Cook County, Illinois Sheriff's Deputy Pattie Nagel, who lost her partner in 1992. I thank her for her kindness and her inspiration.

The chapter Truth, Justice and Badge #4699 could not have been written without the help of the courteous and informative people at the Court Reporter Administration of the First Judicial District of Pennsylvania. To that same end, I am also deeply indebted to the websites www.justice4danielfaulkner.com and www.danielfaulkner.com, specifically to Mr. Paul Palkovic, who was most helpful.

Thanks, appreciation, and tremendous respects are eternally due to Mrs. Maureen Faulkner for her trust, her guidance, her generosity, and, above all, her unflappable courage.

Lastly, gratitude and love must go to my devoted parents, and my two beautiful sisters.

FOREWORD

At 4:00 a.m. on December 9, 1981, my life was changed forever. On that morning, a remorseless killer named Mumia Abu-Jamal violently and callously murdered Officer Daniel Faulkner, my husband of 13 months. Since that day, while Jamal has written his books and waged his campaign of misinformation about Danny's murder, becoming wealthy and famous in the process, I have fought to keep him on Death Row and to keep Danny's memory alive. My struggle to see justice done has afforded me the opportunity to come in contact with many fantastically supportive and insightful people who seem to have an innate ability to understand what I, and every other survivor of a murdered law enforcement officer, has gone through. Gabriel Nathan is one of those rare and wonderful people.

Prior to our first conversation, Gabriel had sent me a draft copy of his book, "For A Tin Star". He told me that he would like my input, and I was happy to oblige. I sat at home alone on a Saturday morning and I was instantly captivated by the stories he told of people like myself. People who had lost loved ones who had been members of America's law enforcement family, to murder. Stories of love, loss, grief, sorrow, and struggle. His stories were about people who are nearly always forgotten by the press after the eye-catching spectacle of a full dress funeral has passed. People who are left to pick up the shattered pieces of their lives in silence and learn to live without a husband, a wife, a father, a mother, a sister, brother or a child. Gabriel Nathan's writing displays a rare insight into a world that I, and others like me, know far too well.

I have always counted myself among those who believe that things, good or bad, happen for a very specific reason. The purpose of our life experiences may, or may not be, revealed to us. Having read his book, and while speaking to Gabriel for the first time, I found myself thinking that this theory was once again proven correct. When Gabriel was a young boy, a collection was taken up at school to benefit the family of a police officer who had been recently slain. A young Gabriel Nathan, like many young people, could not fully grasp the very real circumstances of this tragedy. Though his pocket held a small amount of spare change, he stood motionless as the collection cup passed by. Years later, as he began working on "For A Tin Star", an enlightened and mature Gabriel Nathan found himself looking back on the memory of his inaction that day, many years earlier. I can't help but thinking that the family of that fallen Officer would be so very proud to know that his memory was a driving force behind this wonderful book.

As if lured by the song of a Siren, certain members of the world's media, the political left and the entertainment community, are drawn to America's prisons. They are drawn to these warehouses of the wicked, in search of writers, painters, poets and philosophers. They seek to make news with, or special interests out of, these allegedly "talented" criminals, especially those who inhabit Death Row. Gabriel Nathan is a different type of writer, on a different type of crusade. His cause and his mission are of much greater value to society. By writing this book, Gabriel keeps alive the memory of the thousands of officers who have given their lives for the benefit of each of us.

I have little doubt that given the time and space to do so, Gabriel would tell each and all of their stories.

The murder of a police officer is always big news. Hundreds were slaughtered again last year. The lives of the slain officer's survivors, however, more often than not, go unnoticed by the media, the college community and the entertainment industry. "For A Tin Star" gives each of us the opportunity to gain insight into the aftermath of the violent crimes committed by America's "cop killers". Once you have read this book, you will understand who the real victims are in each of these senseless tragedies.

Maureen Faulkner

A memorial to Lower Merion Township, Pennsylvania Police officer Edward M. Setzer. Efraim Nathan, photographer.

HONOR, INTEGRITY, SERVICE

{a preface}

"IT'S A GREAT LIFE. YOU RISK YOUR SKIN CATCHING KILLERS AND THE JURIES TURN THEM LOOSE SO THEY CAN COME BACK AND SHOOT AT YOU AGAIN. IF YOU'RE HONEST, YOU'RE POOR YOUR WHOLE LIFE. AND, IN THE END, YOU WIND UP DYING ALL ALONE ON SOME DIRTY STREET. FOR WHAT? FOR NOTHING. FOR A TIN STAR."
— *Lon Chaney;* as ex-Sheriff Martin Howe in the film, "High Noon".

As an eight year old child at Penn Wynne Elementary School, I have a vague, almost non-existent memory of my gym teacher, Ms. Deasey, coming around the class one day with a coffee tin to collect donations. Truthfully, I do not remember whether I contributed or not— probably not, (I wasn't very into charity as an eight year old, as I recollect), and I am not even sure I understood exactly what the donations were for. Ms. Deasey explained that she was collecting donations for the Setzer family. Although I did not care very much at the time, the Setzer family was broken, a young wife was now a widow, and three children had been robbed of their right to grow up with their father, all because some career-criminal did not want to go back to jail. A man who, today, is remembered as warm, funny, intelligent, and dedicated, Lower Merion Township, Pennsylvania Police Officer Edward M. Setzer was gunned down, and his family needed help, even the help of elementary school students like myself. Sadly, as an eight year old child who knew nothing of policemen, living or slain, this all meant very little to me.

Eleven years later, at a beautiful ceremony, my township's public safety building was named in Edward Setzer's honor. It was held, fittingly, on May 15th. This day is National Peace Officers Memorial Day, which was signed into law in 1962 by President John F. Kennedy. The event was held at one o'clock in the afternoon, as I remember, and the springtime sun was absolutely brilliant. Members of the Lower Merion Police Department stood on the steps of the police building lined up in three rows. They stood at attention for the duration of the ceremony, white dress-gloves adorned their hands and black morning stripes covered the center of their badges. These acts demonstrated respect for the slain officer, and his widow and three children, all in attendance this day.

The police department's Superintendent spoke, as did many other important officials. Funny and touching stories were told about Officer Ed Setzer, tales were told of the pranks he had pulled, and the people he had helped during his all-too-short life. One police officer remembered that after hearing of Officer Setzer's death he blindly drove home, stumbled through his front door and collapsed in his hallway, crying inconsolably. A set of bagpipes, played by Lower Merion Police Sergeant Collins wailed as inconsolably as that officer had, all those years ago. "Amazing Grace" was in the air in Lower Merion once again but now, eleven years later, it was a slightly less sad sound. A marching band played at the ceremony that afternoon, too. One of the members of that marching band was Edward Setzer's son, all grown up. How proud that father would have been of his son. How proud.

I sat in the third row of the audience at that ceremony, a police memorial pin fastened to my shirt, over my heart. I attached a small piece of black tape across the pin to show respect for the slain officer, and his family. I spoke to Ed Setzer's sister-in-law that afternoon. Noticing my pin, she asked me what organization I was affiliated with— why I was there. I responded, (somewhat embarrassed that I was not affiliated with any organization), that I was simply a citizen of the township and that I was there to pay long overdue respects to Officer Setzer. I don't think she believed me. It was the very least I could do, I thought, especially after I had so callously ignored the coffee-tin in gym class when I was just a boy. I still have not forgiven myself for that inconsiderate, uncaring act, even if it was simply the act of a child.

I suppose that is part of the reason why I decided to write this book— because, every day, thousands upon thousands of young men and women leave their homes and their families to protect our homes and our families, and we don't give them a second thought. For the most part, we, as citizens, do not take the time to thank police officers properly, to graciously acknowledge their sacrifices. This book is my way of saying "thank you". This is my way of giving police officers that much-deserved second thought.

Over the years, doing research for this book and reading about the lives, and the deaths, of police officers in America, I have come across many stories and learned many things. I have learned that, statistically, one police officer in America dies in the line of duty every 52 hours. I was shocked when I learned that, since the first peace officer was killed in America, (New York City Sheriff's Deputy Isaac Smith, shot down in 1792 while attempting to make an arrest), that over 15,000 officers have fallen in the line of duty. I bitterly had to come to terms with the fact that, despite bulletproof vests and shields and back-up and training, that police officers are not only regular targets, but marked victims. Police officers are also something else— they are human beings. They are human beings who decide, for whatever reasons, to do an incredibly demanding and dangerous job, a job that earns them menial pay and menial respect from most of the public they serve so humbly. The police officer asks for nothing in return for his service and his blood, not even the pay and respect he so unquestionably deserves. Every day police officers stand for, and fall for, a cause as old as the Bible and just as important. That cause is the unflinching, furious pursuit of Justice.

Before this preface began, actor Lon Chaney, (playing the fictional, retired Sheriff in "High Noon"), was quoted. His character summed up the life of a law enforcement officer in a few, penetrating sentences, but his character made one mistake, I believe. The quote said a lot of upsetting, but true, things about the law enforcement profession, but, towards the end of the quote, Chaney's character says that the life of a lawman is all "for nothing". That is where I feel that the script is in error. It is most definitely not for nothing. I am sure, to many police officers, it may feel that way quite a lot of the time, but the honor, integrity, and service of peace officers all across America is appreciated and respected by a great many people, but, sadly, not enough. The sacrifices and the losses suffered by the great police family is just simply not adequately understood by many families, like mine, and many people, especially young people, like me.

It is my hope that this book serves to promote a positive and honest portrayal of a part of policing that does get attention but usually when it is too late. The part of policing that I am going to portray for you in this book is the end of a police officer's life. I want you to understand the pain, the anger, the suffering, the agony; and then I want you to be somewhat pro-active. I want you to close the cover on this book, get up out of your chair or your sofa, walk out your front door, and make others understand. You see, this book may be dedicated to police officers and their families, but it was not written for them. This book was written for you, the person who has the potential to change others. I wrote this book for, well, me in a sense— the kid who passed the coffee-tin on to the next child without putting in his nickel. Well, I'm sure that, as you are reading these words, somewhere in Kansas or Florida or California or Ohio, the bagpipes are wailing and the sirens are screaming, and that coffee-tin is coming on down the line again and, kiddo; it's time to put your nickel in.

— G.L.N.

Westchester County, NY Police Memorial Sculpture. Photograph property of Richard Masloski, photographer and sculptor.

BLEEDING BLUE

"Every time a car pulls alongside you, you eye the guy. He thinks you're waiting to catch him going through a red light, but you're waiting to see if he'll pull a gun and start shooting at you."
— *NYC Patrolman James Liedy; excerpted from Robert Daley's book Target Blue.*

Many words and numbers are bandied about over police radios every hour of every day, all across the country. Since a police department is an organization with many strict hierarchies, each call that goes over a police radio is prioritized, according to a pre-determined hierarchy of its own. For instance, an "armed robbery in progress" call will get a fast response from several police units, while a mere "disorderly conduct" call may not get an immediate response and sometimes only one unit will respond. Some departments prioritize their radio calls differently, but there are two words that will send every available police cruiser tearing through the streets, no matter where or when the call goes out. This specific call is referred to numerically in different ways in different departments. For some, the call goes out as an "11-99". In New York City, to cite one example, when this call is broadcast, it is a "10-13". The numbers may be different, but those numbers are usually followed by those two words, mentioned earlier. When those two words are heard over the radio, every police heart is seized and every police foot slams down the accelerator, almost driving it through the floor of the car. There are those words that every police officer prays he will never hear called out, or perhaps have to breathlessly call out himself:

"OFFICER DOWN"

Many times, these words are screamed into police radio mics by horrified back-up officers who arrive on-scene seconds too late. Too late to stop the madman who decided to shoot it out with the young officer on the beat, rather than go back to jail. Too late to stop the back-shooting assassin, out for a cop, out for blood. Too late to fire first. Too late.

Their cars screech to a stop, several units arriving almost simultaneously, from each surrounding street. In the midst of the revolving red and blue lights, the spotlamps and headlights, they see the supine figure on the ground. It is illuminated in a surreal glow as the multicolored lights spill over the body, mixing with its blood— their blood. They are all yelling incoherent cries for help into their radios, all running flat out by this time, running to the aid of their fallen friend, their brother or their sister. As they run, dispatch tries to calmly direct more units and rescue ambulances to the scene. The command "Assist the Officer" can be heard over the radio, but it is a command that need not be given.

Within minutes the scene of the atrocious crime is one of insane and rage-filled chaos, the area is flooded with police cars and ambulances. Usually, by this time, the fallen officer is no longer there. His fellow officers sometimes cannot bring themselves to wait for the ambulance, and the fatally wounded patrolman will be placed gingerly into the back-seat of a police car which will roar away to the closest hospital. The dying officer's blood flows as freely and as unabashed as the tears of the policemen that are riding with him in that car. Sometimes the police officer will die in the back-seat of that police car, cradled in the arms of the men and women he worked with. Sometimes he will die at the hospital, and sometimes he will be dead even before he is placed inside the car. Dead or not, the officer at the wheel will break every traffic law known to man to get that bleeding cop to the emergency room faster than if he were inside a rocket—because there is always room for a miracle. There is always room for hope. But trembling hands pressed down on gaping bullet wounds just can't always stop the blood, and sometimes 120 miles per hour just isn't always fast enough.

Most situations that result in the murder of a police officer begin innocently enough. There are, of course, the blatantly dangerous situations that policemen encounter where they know that the risk of death is considerable, such as a bank holdup or a shooting, however, most officers who are murdered die doing things that, in their lives, may seem relatively innocuous. Traffic-stops, many times for minor offenses, often erupt into deadly confrontations. The subject in the vehicle might have outstanding warrants for his arrest and does not wish to get caught. People in these situations can get so hysterical that they think that if they can just get rid of this one cop, that they will be home free. The officer usually approaches the vehicle having very little idea of what he is going to encounter when he reaches the window. Sometimes, he never even gets to speak his opening line, "Good day, sir. License and registration, please". Sometimes he is shot down before he even gets to see the driver's face. Dallas, Texas Police Officer Robert Wood was killed in this exact manner on the 28th of November, 1976. It was late in the evening and the car that Wood had stopped did not have its headlights on. Speculation was that Wood was just going to give the driver a warning, because he had left his ticket-book on the front seat of his patrol car. He was shot six times.

Robert Wood was killed, it turns out, by a man who had a violent past. However, even officers coming up against regular citizens are just never safe, as was exhibited in Cincinnati, Ohio on the 1st of September, 2000. District 5 Officer Kevin C. Crayon had observed a gentleman getting into a Ford Taurus who just looked too young to be driving a car. Officer Crayon's suspicion was correct, the driver was a 12 year old boy. Flooring the car, with Officer Crayon's hands inside, desperately trying to stop the boy, he sped off. Officer Crayon, father of three, was dragged over 800 feet before managing to unholster his weapon and shoot the driver in the chest. At this point, Crayon was thrown from the car to his death. Officer Kevin C. Crayon, like many other police officers who have been killed in vehicular assaults, was left to die "all alone on some dirty street", just like Lon Chaney said.

Domestic calls, simple family disputes, are also often lethal for police officers. The perpetrator of the abuse resents the presence of the arbitrator, this foreign entity who is trying to involve himself in private, "husband-and-wife-stuff". Many times one or both of the parties involved in the domestic assault will turn against the police officer and attack him, for whatever reason. Chesterfield, South Carolina Sheriff's Deputy Jonathan W. Crawley died in the middle of a domestic abuse incident on the 31st of August, 1998. He was serving papers to remove a husband from his home for assaulting his wife. Before the abusive husband could be expelled from the premises, he managed to shoot both his wife and the Deputy. Sheriff's Deputy Jonathan W. Crawley was twenty six years old.

Arrests, even those made for petty crimes, are extremely dangerous. It is during these moments when the officer is in bodily contact with the suspect where anything can happen.

Although it may appear that the officer is in complete control, he is on top of the suspect who lies, apparently complacent on his stomach, many things can, and do go wrong. Before a suspect is patted down for weapons, he can rapidly produce a concealed gun or knife and kill the officer with it. Also, it is during arrests that officers are often shot with their own guns. During a violent struggle, while the officer is attempting to control the wildly flailing hands of a suspect, the officer's gun can be grabbed and used against him, all within a matter of seconds. That is how Lower Merion Township, Pennsylvania Police Officer Edward M. Setzer died, during a struggle with a burglary suspect. On September 30th, 1988, the suspect wrestled Setzer's weapon away from him and shot him in the chest. Ed Setzer was the third Lower Merion Township officer to have died in the line of duty since the department was established.

Even when suspects are handcuffed and are "securely" locked in the back-seat of a radio police car, two recent cases prove that police officers are simply never truly safe. May 19th, 1998 was a black day in Tampa, Florida, where three peace officers were murdered, all by the same man. Detectives Ricky Joe Childers and Randy Scott Bell had their man. The suspect had just killed his three year old child, but he was all locked up, and handcuffed in the back-seat of their vehicle. As Childers and Bell were transporting the suspect, he used a small key he possessed to unlock his handcuffs. He surprised the Detectives, got control of one of their guns, and killed both of them in a matter of seconds. Later on that day, the same suspect killed Florida State Trooper James Brad Crooks with a rifle he had stolen from the Detectives' squad car. Trooper Crooks was twenty three and had been on the job for nine months. The suspect later committed suicide after a standoff at a gas station.

Two years later, on the 8th of August, St. Louis, Missouri Police Officer Robert Stanze had a suspect handcuffed and ready to go, in the back-seat of his police car. This suspect had already shot another policeman, so Stanze was sure to be extra careful, but even he did not discover the suspect's expertly hidden handgun. The suspect shot and killed Officer Stanze through the police car's window. Another officer, who had been standing outside talking with Officer Stanze, opened fire on the suspect, wounding him. At the time that this sentence is being written, Officer Stanze's wife is expecting twins.

Then there are other cases, fortunately they are nowadays in the minority. There has been no crime committed, there is no investigation in progress, there is no call, there is just a cop or two, strolling along the street in the comforting breeze of a spring day. Or sometimes it is a policeman sitting in his patrol car, catching up on some paperwork. Perhaps a vision of an old partner or his wife flashes before his eyes the instant before he is hit. If the assassin is a good shot, the unsuspecting police officer will feel nothing as the lightning-fast bullet machetes its way through his heart or his skull. However, if the assassin is unskilled in the brutal execution of his crime, or if he wants his victim to know pain before he dies, that officer will see, hear, and feel everything his killer wants him to. He will know immeasurable agony before his torturer is through with him. Many police officers never get to see the look on their assassins faces as they fire, because the police officer usually has his back turned to his killer—he never sees it coming. It is terrifying that there have been many cases of police assassinations in America's history. Two of those cases occurred in the same city, eight months apart. The first victims were 32nd Precinct New York City Patrolmen Waverly M. Jones and Joseph A. Piagentini. It was the 21st of May, 1971 and Piagentini and Jones were walking back to their radio car after answering a call at the Colonial Park Apartments in Harlem. They would never make it back to their car. Two black "revolutionaries" snuck up behind them in the night and began firing into their backs, because they were cops, and they had to die. Waverly Jones, black like his killers, died instantly, four shots to his head and back. He was thirty two. His twenty eight year old partner, Joseph Piagentini, was shot thirteen times, as he begged his murderers to stop shooting him. He died in the back-seat of the radio-car that tried, in vain, to get him to Harlem Hospital alive. On the 27th of January, 1972, New York City lost another black-and-white patrol team, the partnership of 9th Precinct Patrolmen Gregory Foster, 23 and Rocco Laurie, 22. They were both ambushed and assassinated in an eerily similar way to Jones and Piagentini as they walked together down Avenue B.

Although the "revolutionary" idea of killing police officers as a symbol of African American rage basically died out in the 1970s, police officers continue to be lured into situations just to be killed. On the 20th of April, 1995, two peace officers were killed in New Jersey. Haddon Heights Police Officer Richard Norcross, and Camden County Prosecutor's Office Investigator John McLaughlin, were on their way to serve trans-sexual Leslie Nelson with a warrant. But Nelson knew the officers were coming back, because they had been there earlier that day and, when they returned, she was lying in wait. As the lawmen climbed the stairs leading to Nelson's bedroom, John McLaughlin looked up. He saw Nelson standing at the top of the stairs with an AK-47 clutched in her hands. McLaughlin screamed a warning to the officers behind him on the stairs, before he was executed by Nelson. Richard Norcross was shot several times, but managed to escape the house. The other officers ran out of the house, and

Nelson ran to her bedroom window. It was there that, acting as a sniper, she shot Officer John Norcross in the head, who had responded to the scene as a backup officer. Nelson was arrested after a fourteen hour standoff. Somehow, Richard Norcross survived the ambush. His brother, John, did not. Leslie Nelson was tried, and sentenced to death for the murder of Norcross and McLaughlin.

Good shot or bad, slain by thief or assassin, it makes little difference in the end, for a police officer has died. Statistically, one police officer dies every other day in this country. The deep blue ranks have been thinned by one, but at least that officer's pain is over and now, if he was married, a whole other wave of pain has not yet begun. Somewhere in America, there is a young woman sitting on a sofa, watching television. Maybe she is tucking several young ones into bed, or maybe she is just waiting for her husband to arrive home from work, and she will fly to the door to answer it. Her husband won't be arriving home from work tonight, but there will be someone at her door, and she will answer it. She must. It is a knock she was destined to answer the moment her husband raised a white-gloved hand at a ceremony and said the words, "I swear". It is a knock she was destined to answer the moment she said the words, "I do" under a white veil at another ceremony, probably not so long ago.

THE WAIL OF THE WIDOW

"HE LOOKED DOWN AT ME AND SAID IN A WHISPER, 'I'M SORRY, HE'S GONE,' AND THEN HE JUST WALKED AWAY. I SAT THERE UNTIL THE REALITY OF THOSE WORDS REGISTERED IN MY MIND FOR THE FIRST TIME, AND THEN I SCREAMED."

— *Maureen Faulkner;* widow of Philadelphia Police Officer Daniel Faulkner.

A sharp, staccato rapping on the front door at some obscene hour of the night is enough to scare anyone— but a knock at such a time scares nobody more than the person who is the spouse of a police officer. The knock is persistent, this door must be answered. The woman, many times barely into her twenties, sleepily and anxiously makes her way towards the front door, her hand gently brushing against the dark walls. She does not want to turn the lights on, because there are usually young children sleeping soundly in these houses with the knocking on the door.

As she approaches the door, she may notice one of two things. First, she may notice the shape of a policeman's cap in the shadows outside. Or she may notice the lights— blue and red— twirling, flashing and dancing incessantly in the night, signaling just as ominously as church-bells, that a man has died tonight. When the young woman sees either of these sights, her stomach will pucker, perhaps as if she were hit right in the gut. This is not right. This is very wrong. It is just something she knows, that she is no longer a wife, that now

The family of slain Camden County Prosecuter's Office Investigator John McLaughlin. Photograph property of the Philadelphia Daily News, Jim MacMillan, photographer. 27 April, 1995

she is a widow. Now. Not at two in the morning when the shotgun blast sent her husband flying through the air like a thrown sugar-sack, but now, as she fiddles with the locks that separate her from the cruel news she already instinctively knows. Now.

The door opens, somehow, and there they stand, the messengers, the sorrowful angels. They are not messengers from God, but messengers dispatched by their superiors to do a terrible job, probably more emotionally arduous than any crisis-call. Usually, these poor messengers are two uniformed police officers, from the deceased officer's department. These officers will do their absolute best to force their faces to appear vacant and dutiful, so that the young woman can read nothing from their expressionless stares. Of course, she doesn't need to because, standing between those two officers is usually a police chaplain. His face is most likely compassionate and world-weary and he is perhaps pondering the benefits of some other, less taxing occupation at this very moment.

"Mrs. _____? You have to come with us to _____ Hospital. I'm afraid your husband's been involved in an accident." Those are usually the words, more or less, that are to be uttered to the frightened, confused, soon-to-be-destroyed woman as she stands in her doorway. Whether her husband was hit by a car, stabbed in the heart, or shot in the face, she is almost always told that there has been "an accident". Many times, however, the death was not an accident, but she does not know that now, and her visitors intend to keep it that way— for now, at least.

The young woman is allowed time to dress and, if she has children, to call a neighbor or relative to come care for the children. She is then escorted out into the austere darkness for the beginning of what will be the most terrifying and terrible night of her life. Inside the police car, nobody speaks. The radio is usually shut off for fear that information regarding her husband's "accident" will be broadcast. They want her to know nothing that will make her hysterical. It is an imperfect procedure, but, then again, there is no perfect way to accommodate this horrible situation.

The patrol car's red and blue lights turn gloomily in the night, their beautiful colors bouncing off buildings and houses, letting everyone know that things are not as they should be tonight, that the natural order of things has been altered tonight, that the young woman in the back-seat of this car is a widow tonight.

As the police car approaches the hospital where this woman's husband has been brought, the scene is one of madness. Cars are thrown around haphazardly, facing this way and that, practically clogging the street. There are news vans and reporters, limousines and politicians, and, of course, police cars and policemen. Some of them are simply standing there, immobile, awaiting the arrival of the widow. Other officers are openly angry, kicking their cars in frustration and rage. A couple officers outside may have blood on their uniforms. These are the officers who brought the wounded policeman to the hospital. Their faces are most likely white and their eyes are most likely red. These were probably the officers who responded to the initial call first. What horrors they must have encountered as their cars skidded to a halt at that crime scene one can only imagine.

Sick of not being told anything concrete, the widow may leap out of the police car before it even stops, rushing into the hospital. There are people talking to her, calling out her name, asking her stupid questions she does not know the answers to, and they are all reaching for her. She searches for family who probably have not arrived yet. The woman looks left and right and she wants one thing— to see her husband. Usually, at this time, she does not know for sure that he is dead.

There are policemen everywhere, it seems. Some have their sleeves pushed up and wear bandages on their arms, for they have just given their blood for this woman's husband. It does not matter to them if they are her husband's blood type or not, for police officers, their blood is all the same; it is all blue. They look at her in sympathy as she flies on past them. They may not all know her personally, but they all know who she is the second they see her. She wears no name-tag, she is not yet clad in black, but they can tell she is the widow just by looking at her. It is something in her eyes, to be sure— that lost, terrified, panic-stricken look. They can only be the eyes of a young girl, prematurely bereft of the man she barely even got the chance to love. They are the eyes of a young woman who will never be young again.

She waits in a small, somber room for what seems like eternity. Again, she is told little or nothing at all. She paces anxiously, ferociously even, not knowing what to do with herself. She waits like an actor in the wing— craving, pulsing to go out and see what's happening. For a while, it seems like her cue may never come, but it always does. It is usually the police chaplain who has to utter the unforgettable words, sometimes it is the head of the police department, other times it is the mayor, sometimes it is even the presiding O.R. doctor who was just working furiously to save the officer's life. But, whomever is unfortunate enough to be the one to deliver the awful news, the horror, surrealism, and gravity of that moment is forever etched in their brain.

After the young woman has been told that her husband has passed away, the world comes crashing down around her ankles as if the very ceiling of that hospital had caved in. There are condolences offered, some sincere, some not, there are also invariably offers of sedatives. She can hardly think straight enough to refuse or accept them. All she can do is scream. It is the wail of the widow and, to be sure, it can break even the hardest heart. She still wants to see her husband. She is rebuffed. She insists. She does not understand why they will not let her into to view her husband's body. She knows that her husband is dead, but she does not know that both her husband's eyes were shot out by brutal assassins, as Patrolman Gregory Foster's were. She does not know that her husband's chest cavity had to be opened up so that doctors could manually massage his heart. There is tremendous pressure when a police officer is wheeled into the Emergency Room, because a frail young wife is not the only person waiting with baited breath outside those doors. Dozens of angry, hysterical armed men and women are waiting too. No doctor wants a police officer dying on his table. The woman does not know that, minutes ago, a dedicated physician caressed her husband's heart in his hands, praying it would beat again. It would never beat again.

Eventually, once the officer's body is in a presentable state, the widow is finally brought in. There are almost always police officers present at this time in case the widow gets too emotional, touching or kissing the body too much. If there is to be no viewing, this is the last time the young woman will ever see the man who shared her bed, her house, her love, and her secrets. Many times, the widow needs to be gently restrained by the heartbroken officers in attendance, and eventually escorted out of the room. In the inexorable sadness and insanity of the moment, she may even forget to say "goodbye".

And, with that, the shattered widow is returned to her hollow house, devoid forever of the burly laughter and bad jokes made by the powerful, kind-eyed young man in the brown armchair. She knows that, if there are children sleeping upstairs, that she, and no one else, will have to explain to them what has happened to their father. Ironically, it is so incomprehensible that she cannot even begin to explain it to herself. She knows that, while she may lie in her bed, she will not sleep, perhaps not for days, perhaps longer. She knows that, even after all the horror she just endured, this is only the beginning. There are years of pain, emptiness, and sadness ahead. But, before all that agony can even begin, her husband, who lived a hero and died a hero, must now be buried as one.

Thousands of officers salute the casket of slain N.YC. Patrolman Joseph A. Piagentini. Robert Walker/NYT Pictures. 26 May, 1971.

GATHERING KNIGHTS

"BEAR THESE HEROES UP ON THEIR SHIELDS AND, WITH PIPES SLOW AND DRUMS LOW, PROCLAIM THEIR DEEDS TO ALL MANKIND."
　　　　—Sean Ross; Honolulu Metropolitan Police Officer, (retired).

E very culture in the world has specific and varied ways in which their dead are laid to their eternal rest. Customs are followed, traditions are acknowledged, and supreme respect is always given to the immediate family of the deceased. The police culture deals with its fallen according to custom and tradition, just like any other culture. While each department has its own ceremonial permutations, by and large, the police funeral is held in basically the same manner in every state in the union. The ceremony is grandiose in every sense of the word, because the sacrifice that has been made is grandiose, in every sense of the word.

What is immediately striking to the civilian observer is the enormous amount of mourners present. They may not all be wearing blue, they may not all be in uniform, but they are almost all police officers. To give an idea of how well-attended police funerals are, a "small" police funeral will see around five to eight hundred officers gathered to mourn. A "large" police funeral will have anywhere from one thousand to five thousand, all the way up to ten thousand police officers present— sometimes there are even more. When an officer is killed in a small-town or suburban department, many times the closest city department will take over command of the funeral services, to alleviate the burden from the bereaved department. Officers from other departments will cover shifts so that all the officers from the slain policeman's department can attend his funeral, so that the mourning can properly take place.

They come from every corner of the country, even from Canada and England. When word gets out that a police officer has fallen in the line of duty, all available officers rush to his or her funeral to show support, concern, and love. There is an unalterable solidarity that comes with policing. Indeed, it is like a marriage but, instead of two becoming one, hundreds of thousands become one. They are all nameless and faceless to each other, they are all one and the same thing. They are brothers and sisters, united by the gleaming piece of metal that rests above each of their hearts. When one of them goes down, every officer standing at attention outside that church knows that it could have been her, or him. That is why they come. That is why they will always come.

The ranking officer on duty at the funeral is usually responsible for forming the officers in rank outside whatever house of worship the ceremony is taking place in. They stand, wounded but proud and not only are they standing, but they are taking a stand, just by being there. They are taking a stand against the senseless, cowardly butchery that ends the lives of good, young police officers almost every day in this country. This impenetrable army, these gathering knights stand as a warning to the murderers who perpetrated the deed that killed this officer that they mourn today. This wall of lawmen is a message to the killers, speaking loud and clear though the officers themselves stand silent. You can see the message on each of their faces, "You thought you could get out of your trouble by killing a police officer? Think again. You got one of us, but now back-up has arrived. Now you're going to have to kill all of us". It is perhaps because of this, perhaps not, that the majority of people who kill police officers are caught relatively quickly. Most cop-killers simply can't beat the odds.

Since very few houses of worship are big enough to accommodate such an immense number of mourners, the majority of the officers in attendance at the funeral must stand outside while the service is being conducted. Recently, some wealthier and more resourceful police departments have commandeered ampitheaters, high-school gymnasiums, even football stadiums in order to provide for the throng of officers who have come to grieve. But, usually, the majority of police officers in attendance at the funeral must remain outside, standing.

So the officers are lined up, several rows deep, sometimes as many as ten, outside the church. The officers at this funeral have most likely done this before, but it does not get any easier. They are hurt and they are angry and, especially if the killer has not yet been apprehended, they are itching to jump back in their cars and get him. Not only are officers emotionally vulnerable during this time, they are still very much in danger.* Many times the line of officers waiting outside stretches on for a mile in either direction. There they will stand, regardless of whether God decides to shower this heartbreaking scene with driving rain, pelting ice, or blinding sun.

The widow arrives in a limousine as black as her dress and her heart and she may need assistance getting into the church. Her children, if there are any, are with her. The little ones might not fully understand what is happening, but the older ones know all too well what all this means. The widow's family, and the family of her husband come next. Perhaps the

---

*On 22 October, 1970 in San Francisco, California an anti-personnel time-bomb exploded outside a church, sending shrapnel flying into police officers gathered to mourn a patrolman who had been murdered during a bank robbery.

saddest part of the police funeral, if there is a "saddest" part, is the middle-aged couple, looking fit themselves, their faces a mixture of sorrow and disbelief that, again, the natural order of the world has been confused. Their sweet young daughter-in-law is a widow, and they are burying their son.

Now the wait for the hearse begins. Everyone is assembled, the chaplain, the mayor, the widow, the children, and all those officers, all lined up, biting their lips, grinding their teeth, clenching their hands, waiting. One person is missing, the slain hero that shall today be laid to rest. They wait as the widow waited at the hospital, only this time the outcome is not uncertain. These people know that the officer is dead, and they know that, no matter how long it takes for that body to arrive, they will wait patiently, respectfully, and bitterly. At last, heads turn gradually. The moment has arrived. Their brother or sister is coming home.

Preceding the hearse is a police escort. This escort usually consists of two or more police motorcycles, their emergency lights flashing on and off, moving at an infinitely slow pace. However, the escort is sometimes a police car, several police cars, or even a rider-less horse, boots reversed in the stirrups, signifying that this officer will never ride again. The body of the police officer is always under some sort of watch. At the funeral home, if there is to be a viewing, an honor guard of officers will stand at both ends of the casket, to protect their slain brother from some further assault, as if to pay penance of some sort for not being there to save him the night he died.

The police honor guard is waiting for the hearse and, when it arrives, they are more than ready. They have practiced this drill many times, they have gone through the funeral ritual, but each time is like the first. Many times, a department will assign random officers to serve as pall-bearers, but an officer's family can select officers that were close with the dead officer to fulfill the grim and painful duty. As soon as the flag-draped casket is hoisted up on their six strong shoulders, a command will be shouted out. Simultaneously, as if pulled by one gigantic, invisible string from the Heavens, thousands of white-gloved police hands will snap instantly to thousands of black-brimmed police hats in severe salute. The officers will salute until the casket is marched out of their view. Many times, a police bagpiper will play his haunting melody as the casket is carried in. When a set of bagpipes is being played, it is not something that can easily be forgotten. The instrument has the unique ability to send shivers racing up and down the spine all throughout duration of the song, and after. Perhaps it is the circumstances under which they are being played, but perhaps it is some innate sadness, some underlying power that lies deep within that tartan bag. It is not pretty music, nor is it supposed to be. It is more of a signal, an unmistakable signal that now the official period of grieving can commence.

Inside the church, jam-packed with police officers, politicians, friends and relatives, speeches are made. The police chaplain will usually make a beautiful speech celebrating the officer's life, not the events surrounding his death. He will praise the young man for his decision to become a policeman, the very choice that led ultimately to his death. He will call for calm, peace, and love. He will tell the congregation that he understands the pain that the officers are going through, and he does. The chaplain urges the officers to be professional, to be always mindful of their duties and their oaths, and their God.

Many times the mayor will speak. If he is sympathetic and compassionate, his speech will probably be a plea to the community to rally around the broken officers seated and standing before him, to support and honor them for the work that they do and the sacrifices they make. He will speak in glowing terms of the officer encased within the casket even though, most of the time, he never met him. Many times, he will ask the policemen to applaud the fallen officer, or his widow, or both, and he is always obliged. Thousands of white gloves pound against each other in a thunderous ovation that even the most legendary, veteran stage actor will simply never know. The officers standing outside, who are almost always listening to the ceremony through some sort of audio device, clap too.

If the politician is callous and ignorant, he will probably use this moment at the pulpit for self-promotion, citing the need for voters to attend to his issues, such as gun-control, or the placing of more police officers on the street. He will find some way to use today's tragedy as the steppingstone on the way to tomorrow's vote. Then there are the really callous and ignorant politicians— these are the ones who do not even bother to show up. Many times they are on vacation, making speeches elsewhere, or perhaps the circumstances surrounding the officer's death have been hastily deemed "questionable" or "controversial", so the politician is advised to stay away from the funeral and, sadly, sometimes he does. It is perhaps the unwritten policy of many departments, especially large-city departments, to shy away from supporting or publicly grieving for a dead police officer until it is absolutely certain that the officer was not involved in any "suspicious" activities at the time he was killed. Politicians like these will usually send their Deputy-Mayors or even their wives as substitutes at the funeral. Snubbing a police funeral is not only the best way to lose a Fraternal Order of Police endorsement, but, in cities like New York, with thousands upon thousands of law enforcement families voting, it is also a good way to lose an election.

Many times a speech is made by a family member of the slain officer. Sometimes, the entire speech is never heard, because the speaker would have to be superhuman to compose him or herself enough to deliver an entire eulogy at a funeral like this. The poor, demolished family member is often helped, in tears, away from the pulpit and back to their seat, left to put their head in their hands, and wonder how it ever came to this.

Prayers are spoken, sang, and murmured in earnest. Depending upon the religion of the murdered police officer, the religious official will pray in English, Latin, Hebrew, or perhaps even some other language. The tongue of the words spoken over the proud casket is not important. Religion itself, while immeasurably important, pales in comparison to the enormity of the police presence. The officers in those pews are everyone and everything. They are fathers, mothers, brothers, sisters, sons and daughters. Some of them were brought up in idyllic countrysides, some in quaint suburbs, some in threatening cities. They are Catholic, Protestant, Muslim, and Jewish, but their individual religion matters as little as the department they work for today. Today they are not New York City patrolmen, they are not DC Metropolitan police officers, they are not Alabama State Troopers, nor are they Cook County Sheriff's Deputies. Today, they are just cops. A black strip of tape or elastic covers the midsection of their badges, each and every one of them today. This black strip says that there is mourning to be done, but it also says something else— that the grief is universal, that it stretches across state lines. That black strip covers the department insignia or state seal on every badge at this funeral to show that there are no departments, no municipalities today, there are only cops, grieving together, and that is as it should be.

At the ceremony's conclusion, the casket is again lifted high on the pallbearers' shoulders and is carried carefully from the church. As the doors open, the men and women outside salute sharply once again. The bagpipes cry out as if to represent all the pain of this day all over again. The emotionally-spent widow sometimes has to be half-escorted, half-carried down the steps to her waiting limousine. As that limousine's door closes and the car starts to move, she knows that she is in for the longest, most agonizing ride of her life— comparable only to an equally arduous and terrifying ride she took, in the back-seat of a police car, only three-or-so nights before.

The cortege that follows the hearse to the cemetery is so long that entire streets and sometimes highways have to be temporarily closed off so that the procession can proceed unimpeded. The motorcade routinely involves hundreds upon hundreds of police vehicles, each with their high-beams on and their red and blue roof lights all ablaze. It is not uncommon for the procession to stretch on and on for miles. Often, police officers, with supportive civilians right behind them, will be stretched out in lines on either side of the street, saluting the hearse as it goes by. At the head of the procession is usually a very special police car— the vehicle assigned to the slain officer will often be driven, in his honor, to the cemetery. The light-bar on the roof of the car will be draped in rich, black mourning cloth. If the officer was a foot patrolman, or if his own patrol car is riddled with bullet-holes from the attack that ended his life, a random squad car from his department will be used, or this part of the ceremony will be omitted altogether. Newspaper photographers and television news cameramen will go to any length to get the perfect shot of the massive, beautiful procession. They will climb onto building roof-tops, highway overpasses, and bridges just for that one picture, which frequently wins them coveted photojournalism awards. Sometimes, the police officers attending the funeral will walk from the church to the cemetery. This walk can sometimes take miles to complete, but the officers do not seem to mind. For a slain police officer and his family, these officers would walk twice around the globe and back, because they know that any one of them would do it for any other.

Once all of the family-members and officers are assembled together again at the graveside, a brief service is conducted by the police chaplain. "Taps" is played and the flag that draped the policeman's casket is folded, almost religiously, by the honor guard in a taut, perfect triangle. The flag is presented to the head of the police department, who is saluted by the highest-ranking member of the honor guard. He salutes back. He then turns and walks over to where the widow sits. He gets down on his knees, as if to beg her forgiveness for the awful events that brought them to this place today, as if he was personally responsible for her husband's death. The head of the department offers the flag to the widow. She either accepts it gratefully or bitterly—it does not matter. The commissioner whispers kind words into her ear that, despite their good intentions, most likely ring hollow. A three shot volley is performed with great precision by rifle-carrying officers and the bagpipes cry out one last, heartbreaking time.

If there is a cop-killer still to be caught, the officers on duty, working on the case, will get right back into their cars and will try to catch that cop-killer. The officers who are not on duty will most likely get right back into their cars and try to catch that cop-killer. Officers from neighboring departments will express their grief and their sorrow, and will offer every available resource to help catch that cop-killer too. The chilling sounds of the pipes will still be in the officers' heads as they patrol the streets of their towns and cities, eyes peeled for the one who felled their friend.

Every officer who has come from some other department for this funeral will remove his black mourning strip and will do his best never to think of this day again— until the next one. The black mourning tape will remain on the badges of the police officers who worked in the same department as the slain officer for a set amount of time, usually thirty days, but it might as well remain forever, for it can be said that the slain police officer never truly dies. Only if we let him.

TRUTH, JUSTICE, AND BADGE #4699

"TRY AS HE MIGHT, THE BEAUTY OF HIS VOICE CANNOT UNDO THE EVIL OF HIS DEED."

— *Tom Ferrik, Jr. speaking of convicted cop-killer Mumia Abu-Jamal.*

The state of Pennsylvania, where I live, has lost many police officers. As of the writing of this book, 610 law enforcement officers have fallen in the line of duty in this state. Many of the officers who have died in Pennsylvania were employed by the Philadelphia Police Department. In 1980, the year I was born, Philadelphia buried five police officers, Ernest Davis, Garrett Thomas Farrell, Robert Smith, and Officer William Washington who, on January 16th, 1980 was shot and killed as he responded to a call reporting a "man with a gun". Officer Ivan Walker, of the Philadelphia Housing Authority Police Department, was murdered on the 11th of September by the man he was attempting to arrest outside of a senior citizens' home. Numerically speaking, 1980 was a terrible year for Philadelphia police officers. The new year would bring with it fewer officers killed, but the year would prove to be no less terrible.

The scene of the crime. Gabriel Nathan, photographer.

In 1981, two police officers were killed in the line of duty in the city of Philadelphia. The first to die in 1981 was Officer James Mason. Officer Mason was sitting in his patrol car in West Philadelphia when a sniper opened fire on him. A bullet struck him in the head, and Officer Mason died the next day, technically due to cardiac arrest. There are probably very few people today who even know what happened to the man who killed him, and it is doubtful that many people care. In fact, who even knows if the perpetrator of this disgusting crime was ever caught? It just isn't quite fashionable to discuss Officer Mason's case at a dinner party in Center City, or on a street-corner in Germantown. No, nobody ever seems to talk about the day Philadelphia Police Officer James Mason was assassinated. May 10th, 1981 just doesn't seem to mean very much to anyone anymore.

The second, and last, Philadelphia police officer to be killed in 1981 died in much the same way as Officer Mason. A bullet killed him, and he was doing nothing to provoke the assault that ended his life, doing nothing, that is, except his job. At a little before 4:00 in the morning on December 9th, 1981, a police officer wearing badge number 4699 pulled over a battered, blue Volkswagen Beetle for traveling the wrong way down a one-way street with its lights off. The young officer, rapidly approaching his 26th birthday, called the stop in and, being a smart cop, *(already a five year veteran of the force),* he radioed for back-up. The officer exited his police vehicle and, after a short conversation, ordered the driver of the Volkswagen to step out of the car. Several witnesses testified that the driver of the Volkswagen turned and struck the officer in the face. As the officer was trying to subdue and arrest the driver, another man came running up to the scene. The man had a gun. The man leveled his gun at the officer's back from 24 inches away and fired. The assailant's bullet found its mark. The officer, stunned and bleeding, spun around, tore his revolver from his holster, aimed at his assailant's chest, and fired back. The policeman's bullet found its mark. The wounded officer collapsed to the ground face up, the impact of the fall knocking his revolver out of his hand. He lay unarmed, as helpless as a child. His assailant, soon to become his assassin, stumbled over to the prostrate officer and fired several more shots. He then straddled the officer's head, placed the muzzle of his gun not inches from his face, and fired, sending the final bullet careening through that police officer's brain. The murderer then tried to run, but he had lost too much blood, and he fell to the ground several feet away from his victim. As the first responding back-up officers approached the killer and ordered him to "freeze", the killer made a move for his revolver. He was kicked in the throat in an effort to get him away from the gun, and was arrested after a brief struggle. The murdered officer's name was Daniel Faulkner. The murderer's name is Mumia Abu-Jamal.

While nobody knows very much about the circumstances that ended the life of Officer James Mason, everybody, it seems, knows about the circumstances that killed Officer Daniel Faulkner— or at least, they think they do. It is interesting to note that James Mason and Daniel Faulkner were both policemen in Philadelphia, killed the same year, only seven months apart, almost to the day, and yet, there are no newspaper articles written about the James Mason case anymore. Why are there new articles about the Daniel Faulkner case at least once a month, many times more? There is nobody celebrating the murderer of Officer James Mason, so why are there constantly protests and demonstrations and gatherings that celebrate the murderer of Officer Daniel Faulkner? Shouldn't this case have been over and done with years ago? After all, a racially-mixed jury, *(10 whites, 2 African Americans),* deliberated for only five hours before unanimously voting to convict Daniel Faulkner's killer all the way back in 1982. After all, that same jury unanimously voted to sentence Officer Faulkner's killer to death all the way back in 1982. After all, Officer Faulkner's killer himself admitted to the murder on the night he was arrested. In the Emergency Room at Jefferson Memorial Hospital, Jamal was heard to ragefully utter the words, "I shot the motherfucker and I hope the motherfucker dies".* After all, he was found, lying, wounded, not twenty feet from the freshly butchered corpse of Officer Daniel Faulkner at 13th and Locust on that cold December night.

Despite his confession, his bizarre courtroom antics, and his unrepentant disposition, Mumia Abu-Jamal is a celebrity, he is a star. The books he writes sell like hotcakes, his picture is everywhere it seems. His voice can be heard on the radio and, incongruously, at college graduation ceremonies. He writes ceaselessly from his cell on Pennsylvania's Death Row, where he has resided for seventeen years, as of the writing of this book. He has a bigger following than many rock bands, including the bands that hold concerts championing his bid for a new trial, if not his outright freedom. He has actors, musicians, politicians, radicals and reactionaries on his side. Curiously enough, Mumia Abu-Jamal has, never once, offered to explain the events that ended with Officer Daniel Faulkner's murder to all of his rabidly blind fans, followers, and assorted hangersons.

If it is possible for a man to be killed more than once, then Daniel Faulkner has died a thousand deaths. As if it were not bad

---

*It is true that Officer Gary Wakshul did not report hearing this statement until two months later. However, what most Mumia supporters conveniently forget is that Jefferson Hospital Security Officer Priscilla Durham also heard the statement and filed a written report the very next day, 10 December 1981, quoting Jamal directly.

enough that there are tens of thousands of people cheering on the man who took his life, some of those same people insist on defaming Daniel Faulkner's name and memory. They call him a pig, a Nazi, a racist. They call him "Daniel Fuckner". These people know no limits, there is no depth to which they will not sink in their efforts to vilify the brave, young police officer who got shot in the back by a cop-killer. They curse Daniel Faulkner's widow, Maureen, herself only 24 years old when her husband was killed. They have threatened her life. They slander her because she stands up to them, because she knows that Mumia Abu-Jamal shot and killed her husband. They deride her because for every word of unsubstantiated garbage they throw at her, she has facts with which to rebut and they know that, deep deep down, they have nothing. It is mainly because of their abuse that Maureen Faulkner left her home in Philadelphia to take up an unlisted residence in California. During my correspondence with her, packages were mailed to my house in ambiguous-looking security envelopes with no return-address. That is how this woman has been forced to live.

Even Abu-Jamal's despicable former attorney, Len Weinglass, has joined in to bash Mrs. Faulkner. During the trial, when Daniel Faulkner's bloody police uniform shirt was held up in court, Maureen Faulkner claimed that Mumia Abu-Jamal turned in his chair and smiled at her, causing her to weep and be escorted from the courtroom, *(Mrs. Faulkner told me on the telephone that Jamal often smiled at her during the proceedings).* Weinglass asserted that Mrs. Faulkner made that up. Weinglass stated that Mumia was not in court on the day that the uniform shirt was held up in court, essentially labeling Mrs. Faulkner as a liar. However, the following selections from the actual trial transcripts will serve to prove beyond any doubt that Mumia Abu-Jamal most certainly was in court on that day. In this selection, Philadelphia

Police Officer John Heftner, an evidence handler, is asked by Prosecutor Joseph McGill:

McGill: "Would you look at C-27?"

Heftner: "Yes."

McGill: "Can you identify it?"

Heftner: "It's Officer Faulkner's shirt."

(21 June, 1982, T.R. 4.10)

That verifies that the shirt was, in fact, displayed on the 21st of June, 1982. To prove that Mr. Jamal was present in court on that date, I offer another piece of the court trial transcript, this selection taken from the same day, only a few moments later. In the following section of transcript, Joseph Kohn, then the manager of Pearson's Sporting Goods, is asked a question by Mr. McGill relating to Abu-Jamal's gun, a .38 caliber Charter Arms revolver, purchased there.

McGill: "And is there a name indicated on the record as to the purchaser [of that gun]?"

Kohn: "Yes, there is."

McGill: "And what is his name?"

Kohn: "Mumia Abu-Jamal."

McGill: "Would that be Mumia Abu-Jamal?"

Kohn: "That is correct."

McGill: "Is that the individual in the courtroom today?"

Kohn: "Yes, sir, it is."

McGill: "Would you point him out?"

Kohn: "Right there, sir."

(21 June, 1982, T.R. 4.35)

If this is not enough, an article by Marc Kauffman appearing in The Philadelphia Inquirer on the 22nd of June, 1982 mentioned the incident where Maureen Faulkner had to be escorted out of the courtroom in tears.

While Mumia has still never offered his version of what happened on the 9th of December, 1981, Jamal's legal teams have. Their explanations and conspiracy-theories are either absurd, under-developed, and/or implausible but they all have one factor in common; they are all factually unsupported. There is a contention that Officer Faulkner was shot by a mystery man, *(who, after 19 years has still yet to be identified),* who alighted from the passenger side of Cook's Volkswagen. However, Faulkner was facing the Volkswagen as he was shot, and tests done on Officer Faulkner's jacket prove that he was shot from behind. Additionally, the claim that Officer Faulkner was shot by someone other than Mumia Abu-Jamal is rebuked by several eye-witnesses who had never met before that night, never had time to check their stories out with each other, and had no reason to frame Mr. Jamal.

Albert Magilton saw the shooting that night, and he identified Jamal as the shooter as Jamal sat, handcuffed, inside a police wagon, not twenty minutes after police arrived. Michael Scanlon, a visitor to Philadelphia, was driving in his car that night and saw Cook hit Faulkner, and he witnessed the final shot that Jamal fired into Faulkner's face. Scanlon stated that, when Jamal shot Officer Faulkner in the face, Faulkner's *"body jerked. His whole body jerked," (25 June, 1982, T.R. 8.8).* Cynthia White, a prostitute, stated that Jamal *"came on top of the Police Officer & shot some more times. After that he went over & he slouched down & he sat on the curb," (21 June, 1982, T.R. 4.94-5).* All of those witnesses know what they saw. Robert Chobert was also a witness that night, and he most certainly knows what he saw. As he said at the trial, *"I know who shot the cop, and I ain't going to forget it," (19 June, 1982, T.R. 2.56).* Robert Chobert was true to his word, he didn't forget. Thirteen years after he said those words, he was telling the same story to a PCRA committee gathered to determine whether Jamal deserved post-conviction relief. They ruled that he did not deserve post-conviction relief.

Robert Chobert was driving his taxi that night. He had parked to let out his passenger. He could not have chosen a better place to witness a murder. Chobert had parked his cab behind Officer Faulkner's radio patrol car, making him possibly the closest witness to the crime that was about to unfold, right before his eyes. Chobert has identified Jamal as Faulkner's killer on no less than three occasions, but never more dramatically than in this excerpt from Jamal's pre-trial Motion to Suppress hearing. It is interesting to note that here, in early June, Mr. Jamal is asking the questions. Jamal was allowed to act as his own attorney, *(pro-se),* until he abused the right, constantly behaving in a disruptive manner. In order for the case to proceed, Jamal had to be removed as pro-se counsel and he was replaced with his back-up counsel, Anthony Jackson. There are claims by Mumia's supporters that Mr. Jamal was removed unfairly from the courtroom, however, the trial record is replete with instances where Judge Sabo practically begs Jamal to behave, many warnings were given before Jamal was thrown out, and Jamal was allowed the chance to behave himself at the beginning of every new day in court. Mumia's defenders also claim that Jackson was not experienced enough, that this was his first murder case. However, Jamal's friends highly recommended Jackson, and Jackson himself stated at Jamal's post-conviction relief hearing in 1995 that he had tried *"a minimum of 16, perhaps 20 cases, 20 murder cases before Mr. Jamal's case," (7-27-95, T.R. 92-93).* Here, Jamal questions Chobert about exactly what he saw on the night of the murder, the 9th of December, 1981,

Jamal: "You did see the cop being shot - the man shoot the cop?"

Chobert: "Yeah, I said I did, didn't I?"

Jamal: "Well, you sure did. And you saw me in the back of the wagon, didn't you?"

Chobert: "Yes, I did."

Jamal: "What made you sure it was the same man?"

Chobert: "Because I saw you, buddy. I saw you shoot him!"

Jamal: "You saw me-"

Chobert: "I saw you shoot him, and I never took my eyes off you until you got in the back of that wagon."

(2 June, 1982, T.R. 2.74-5)

Some of Jamal's supporters theorize that Faulkner fired first at Jamal. This outrageous conjecture is in direct contradiction to every single eyewitness statement given to police moments after the shooting had occurred. The physical evidence gathered at the scene, the eyewitness statements and subsequent courtroom testimony, tests performed on Officer Faulkner's clothing, as well as Officer Faulkner's police record, *(multiple commendations, but not one single complaint in nearly six years of policing),* speak for themselves quite well with regards to this matter.

There is no doubt that Mumia Abu-Jamal murdered Philadelphia Police Officer Daniel Faulkner in cold blood. There are so many facts which point to Jamal, and only hazy speculation and wild theories that do not— so why are there so many people supporting Jamal? This is a question that has long puzzled me, but I think I may have figured it out. Everybody needs somebody to look up to in life. Mumia Abu-Jamal embodies some wonderful qualities for people all over the world to admire. He is a former Black Panther, a revolutionary, if you will, fighting for justice for oppressed minorities. He is a noted radio journalist, an articulate, eloquent speaker and a highly skilled, powerful writer. Furthermore, he is a handsome, distinguished-looking man, which does not hurt. To his supporters, he was an innocent, shot by a racist cop, beaten and arrested by a cadre of racist cops, beaten again, brought before a racist, cop-loving judge for a sham of a trial, *(which it most certainly was, but only due to Mr. Jamal's behavior),* thrown out of court without cause, and, lastly, convicted and sentenced to death by that racist, cop-loving judge. Of course, many people who are of that opinion are not aware that, under existing Pennsylvania law, the judge does not convict defendants, the jury does. More importantly, especially in this case, the judge does not impose the death penalty, the jury does, and they have to agree unanimously, and that they did. Lastly, it has often been stated that Judge Albert F. Sabo was biased and that he was a "long-standing member" of the Fraternal Order of Police, serving as undersheriff, *(fact memorandum 88).* The actual truth of the matter, found in the text of the appeal court's denial of post-conviction relief for Jamal is that Judge Sabo was only a member of the Fraternal Order of Police for a short amount of time. Furthermore, Sabo resigned from the Fraternal Order of Police when he became a judge—eight years before Jamal's trial, *(N.T. 7/12/95, 17-18).*

Even for that percentage of Mumia's supporters who are smart enough to know that Mumia did, in fact, pull the trigger that night, they believe that Mumia was a warrior, acting in defense of his brother who was being brutally beaten by the fascist pig police of Philadelphia, *(actually, Mumia's brother only sustained a minor cut behind his ear, for which he refused treatment).* Of course, nothing could be farther from the truth. Officer Faulkner was in the process of making a totally legal arrest of William Cook, who had just assaulted the officer, when he was shot from behind by a man who evidently hated Philadelphia police officers long before that night. In fact, since every Mumia supporter around the world feels that he or she is well-informed enough to speak his or her mind about this case, I would now like to offer my opinion of what happened on the night of the 9th of December, 1981, at a little before four o'clock in the morning.

I think it all occurred as I explained earlier, but with one vital twist. As Faulkner was attempting to arrest Mumia's brother, the story goes that Mumia "just happened" to be parked nearby, saw what was happening, grabbed his .38 caliber revolver, rushed to the scene, and fired. That is quite an astounding coincidence, if you think about it, that Mumia just happened to be at the exact intersection at the exact moment his brother was getting arrested— at a little before four o'clock in the morning, out of any place in the city. It is my contention that the murder of 6th District Philadelphia Police Officer Daniel J. Faulkner was not the uncanny coincidence it appeared to be, but that it was quite possibly a carefully planned out, finely orchestrated ambush. Allow me to cite a bit of history to illustrate my claim.

On the 19th of May, 1971, New York City Patrolmen Thomas Curry and Nicholas Binetti observed a Ford Maverick traveling the wrong way down a one-way street. The two patrolmen gave chase and, once they caught up to the car, they pulled up alongside of it and motioned for the driver to pull the car over. The front-seat passenger opened fire on the patrolmen with a submachine gun. Miraculously, both patrolmen survived the attack— barely. The Black Liberation Army claimed responsibility for this attack and others like it. This revolutionary group was a splinter-group of the Black Panthers.

Presumably Mumia Abu-Jamal, having been a member of the Black Panthers himself, would have most certainly been familiar with these planned attacks on policemen. It is also interesting to note that the Black Liberation Army was the only other organization to which Black Panthers could belong to, according to rules and guidelines set up by the Panthers themselves. Curry and Binetti were lured into a trap that night— they were on a rotating security detail, stationed outside of the District Attorney's house in a clearly-marked radio car. The attackers observed the patrolmen carefully and they knew exactly what to do to arouse the patrolmens' suspicions.

Is it so unbelievable to think that Jamal's brother might just have driven his car down that one-way street the wrong way on purpose, to bait Daniel Faulkner into stopping him exactly where he did? Is it really so improbable to believe that a man who believed that police officers were racist and abusive would devise a scheme to trap a police officer and then hunt him down, like an animal in the woods? Is it really so crazy? It isn't any crazier than the claim that Mumia "just happened" to be right around the corner as his brother was duking it out with a Philadelphia police officer. Am I the only one who finds that somewhat interesting? Am I also the only person who finds it somewhat interesting that a witness to the crime, in her statement given to police on the 15th of December, stated that she saw the "Volkswagen go around the block a couple of times that night before the shooting"? I happen to find that extremely interesting. That shows that Cook, the driver of the Volkswagen, was quite possibly trying to arouse Daniel Faulkner's suspicions by driving his car the wrong way around the block "a couple of times" with its lights off, literally forcing Faulkner to stop the car where he did. In all fairness to the other side of the argument, this information is coming from a witness who admitted to being "half a nickel bag high" at the time her statement was given. However, the pure fact of Mumia's appearance at the scene of the traffic stop, his gun already loaded with high-velocity Plus-P ammunition at 3:51 in the morning is just a little too coincidental. I find no way of escaping it— it is very possible that Daniel Faulkner was lured into an ambush. I think that Mumia Abu-Jamal was tired of watching African Americans getting trodden on by police officers, and this was his chance for revenge because, as Jamal himself once said, political power comes from "the barrel of a gun". I think he was a man with a lot of misguided anger and frustrations, and he decided to take out those frustrations on a recently married, Vietnam veteran, decorated police officer named Daniel J. Faulkner.

You may be asking yourself, "why is he writing this?". That is a good question and, when I look at what I am up against, many times I ask myself the same question. I always come up with the same, resolute answer, though. It seems that there is a great silent majority, in the Philadelphia-area especially, who honestly believes that Mumia Abu-Jamal committed this heinous crime. This majority is reluctant to speak, because the minority who supports Mumia shouts them down at every turn, intimidates them, and threatens them. I myself have had my life threatened several times for speaking out against Jamal, *("I think that you should be the one in the chair, not Mumia", are the choice words of one of my attackers),* and I do not expect that particular situation to improve much, but I do not care. Why should I? In fact, ignorant people like the person mentioned above are all the more motivation for me to continue. Pam Africa, a very active member of Mumia Abu-Jamal's publicity machine, is herself one of the ignorant people who motivates me, daily, to continue. To cite one example of the things that she often says that encourage me to continue writing, I offer a selection of a "speech" she gave to thousands of people on May 7th, 2000 at the widely publicized "Day for Mumia", held at Madison Square Garden. Ladies and gentlemen, Pam Africa:

"Who the hell is Danny Faulkner?... We've known who Mumia Abu-Jamal is from the time he exited his mother's womb. Now who the hell is Danny Faulkner? Why is the government so hell-bent on breaking the law that they won't tell us who Danny Faulkner is? I don't know, but I got some heresay.... I heard from reliable sources that this man was a pimp to some black women, teenagers in school.... I don't know, it's heresay. But if you are calling this monster a hero, like we're calling Mumia a hero, then dammit, prove it!... We're demanding to know who's Danny Faulkner!"

Well, they're "demanding to know who's Danny Faulkner" and, since I very much doubt that anybody who could have fairly described Daniel Faulkner was present in the auditiorium that day, I would now like to address Ms. Africa and her inquisitive friends to try and answer her pointed question, "Who the hell is Danny Faulkner?". To the best of my knowledge, Daniel Faulkner was one of six brothers, he also had one sister. At the time he was killed, his mother was a widow. He was in the Vietnam War and when he came home, like many young men, he entered the police academy. Daniel Faulkner graduated second in his class at the academy. During his five-year police career, he won many citations for his work as an officer and received no recorded complaints. Besides being a police officer, Daniel Faulkner was a dedicated husband to a young woman named Maureen. He had only got the chance to be her husband for thirteen months, because he was slaughtered without provocation by Mumia Abu-Jamal. That's who Daniel Faulkner is or, rather, was. And all that I was able to gather just from reading the Philadelphia Inquirer. I don't know why Pam Africa is having such a hard time finding out who Daniel Faulkner was, I found it all relatively easy. I would think that Pam Africa would find it all relatively easy too.

I have taken the time and the great pains to research this case carefully before coming out to state my opinions, and you should too. I have purposefully not included many references from the trial transcript, because that is not my job, that is your job. Do research— I implore you to learn about this case, what really happened that night and what happened at the trial. I do not think that, for instance, many people who profess to be knowledgeable about Daniel Faulkner's brutal murder realize just how fast the events that night occurred. I say this because it is constantly being suggested to me by various Mumia supporters that there was a rather long period of time for somebody else to have killed Faulkner, for police officers to "stage" the scene and coerce witnesses and effectively frame Jamal. The Philadelphia Police Radio Tape Transmittal from Central Division clearly shows us just how fast Daniel Faulkner was executed and how quickly back-up arrived. Daniel Faulkner, assigned to a marked radio police car, (*RPC, in police lingo*), put out this radio call from his vehicle to dispatch at **3:51:08 AM:**

RPC 612*(Faulkner):* "I have a car stopped ah 12, 13th and Locust."

Radio*(Dispatch):* "Car to back 612, 13th and Locust."

RPC 612: "On second thought send me a wagon, 1234 Locust."

After that transmission, Daniel Faulkner got out of his vehicle and approached Cook. According to witness statements, Cook and Faulkner had some sort of altercation, the punch was thrown by Cook, Faulkner used force to defend himself, and was shot from behind and then again while he was on the ground. After being approached by a witness, this radio transmission was broadcast by RPC 601 at **3:52:27 AM:**

RPC 601: "Yeah, we just got information from a passerby, there's a policeman shot a, I think it sounds like it was at 12."

From the time Daniel Faulkner exited his patrol car to the time the "policeman shot" call was put out by RPC 601, no more than 80 seconds had elapsed. After 601's call had been broadcast, it only took Officers Shoemaker and Forbes, the first-responders, nine seconds to arrive on-scene. Nine seconds. That's how fast they got there when they found Daniel Faulkner— blood gushing out of his face— and a cop-killer, sitting there. Just sitting there waiting for them.

So learn for yourself. Learn about the crime. Learn about the trial. Who was disruptive, was it Judge Sabo or Mumia? Who was racist, was it Daniel Faulkner or Mumia? And, most importantly, who killed Daniel Faulkner? The answers to all of those questions and more can all be found in thousands of pages of trial transcript, all of which are available for review at the Office of the Clerk of Quarter Session, located at the Criminal Justice Center, 3rd Floor, 1301 Filbert Street, Philadelphia, PA. 19107. If you are not quite ambitious enough to make the trek, the transcripts are also available on the web at www.justice4danielfaulkner.com, one of the only websites that is dedicated to preserving the memory of Officer Faulkner, and truth behind this case. This site is a source of factually-backed information regarding the slaying of Daniel Faulkner and the conviction of Mumia Abu-Jamal. Two other sites that are in support of Faulkner are www.mumia911.com and www.mumia.net. There are hundreds of pro-Mumia sites for you to choose from for any opposing information.

To be perfectly honest, I do not know what the outcome of this whole horrible mess will be. I do not know if

Pennsylvania's governor will buckle under the enormous political and popular pressure and grant Mumia a pardon or release. I do not know if Mumia's last federal appeal, pending now, will result in a new trial. I do not know if the death sentence imposed upon Mumia Abu-Jamal on the 3rd of July, 1982 will ever be carried out. I do not know if Jamal will ever be made to pay for the ghastly sins he committed on the 9th of December, 1981. I do not know if Maureen Faulkner will ever know the peace and justice that she so deserves. I just don't know anymore. I suppose all I can ask of you is that you try and think for yourself before you take a stand on this issue. I do not ask you to just simply believe me and the facts and words and ideas I have presented you with, you must read more. I ask you to question. Who else could have shot Daniel Faulkner? Why has Mumia never explained what happened that night? Why did Mumia's own brother not appear in Mumia's defense at the trial? How is it possible that Mumia "just happened" to be right there as his brother was getting arrested? Who can explain Mumia's empty revolver at his side? What and where is all this evidence that points to someone else?

The plain fact of the matter is this: Mumia Abu-Jamal shot a young policeman in the back, was in turn shot himself, and as that officer lay on his back, Mumia blasted his head apart. Certain local spin-doctors, Mumia-supporters, lawyers, and agenda-possessing reporters would have you believe that this is a racial case, that what happened on the 9th of December, 1981 was a showdown between the "black assailant" and the "white police officer". I respectfully assert my right to disagree. What happened in the wee hours of the morning that day was an encounter between two men. One was doing his job, and the other was doing murder. One had a Charter Arms .38, and the other had badge #4699.

In Memorium

Police Officer
Jose Manuel Ortiz
03-01-71 to 09-22-00
25th District

The program distributed at the funeral for Philadelphia Police Officer Jose M. Ortiz. 26 September, 2000.

Amongst the Throng

"Dios mio," she cried. My God. Over and over and over again, each time it was uttered, it cut deeper into the hearts of every mourner there. As I sit here typing now I know that all the clattering keyboard keys in the world can not possibly serve to drown out the sounds that anguished, destroyed policeman's mother made as the casket was closed on her son for the last time. I know that, although the three-shot volley was performed approximately three hours ago, that mother is probably still moaning that skyward cry, right this very minute.

Sitting in that church, my friend David Basner on my right, a stranger on my left, and blue everywhere else, I had to shut my eyes as the officer's mother cried. I know now that it made no difference whether I could see her or not; she would still be there, sobbing inconsolably, and the son that she undoubtedly loved more than the sun and the moon would still be dead. I knew that it did not matter, but I just couldn't look anymore. I knew that this day would hurt, but I do not think that I was prepared for it to hurt as much as it did. Everything hurt. It hurt to look his sister, his daughter, and his widow. It hurt to see his body, ensconced deep within in a layer of flowers, prayers, and love. It hurt to see all of the covered badges. It hurt to see the tears, and it hurt to cry them. I was ready for all of this, and yet, I wasn't.

In 1971, the city of Philadelphia had two police officers die— however— it also had one born. Jose Manuel Ortiz was born on March 1st, 1971 and it was obvious, to his family, at least, that he was going to be a cop. He realized his lifelong dream on the 2nd of December, 1996, when he graduated from the Philadelphia Police Academy. He was assigned to the 25th District, (the district in which he was raised), on May 25th, 1997. Noemi Catalla, Officer Ortiz's sister, referred to him as her "hero". Jose M. Ortiz, who lived a hero, died a hero on September 21st, 2000. The majority of this book has been devoted to officers who have been feloniously slain, but the circumstances surrounding Officer Ortiz's death are no less senseless, no less tragic, and no less heart-breaking.

Jose Ortiz was running flat-out, attempting to arrest a suspected car-jacker who made the stupid mistake to run from him. His partner was in their unmarked radio car, attempting to head off the perpetrator. Officer Ortiz called for assistance on his police radio as he ran, in dogged pursuit of his suspect. Assistance came roaring up to the scene, in the form of 25th District Police Officer Tina Hudrick, gunning the engine of her over-worked Ford Crown Victoria, forcing it to barrel down Cambria Street. As Hudrick raced to Ortiz's aide, something went terribly wrong. According to reports, her police vehicle was going at approximately fifty miles per hour when it struck a parked light-blue Cadillac, sending it out-of-control. Her patrol car accidentally slammed into Officer Ortiz, throwing his 29 year old body onto her windshield and onto the pavement. As Ortiz's partner pulled up to the scene, he reportedly asked a dazed and injured Hudrick, "Did you hit my partner?". In her disbelief, she blankly answered, "No, I hit that car over there". Despite her honest denial, as the day wore on the horrifying reality of what truly did occur at 25th and Cambria would come crashing down around Officer Hudrick, the Ortiz family, and every single Philadelphia police officer.

They all went to Temple University Hospital— they did not need to be told— they just all went. They went to check up on their friend, they went to put their arms around his family, to offer them their shoulders, and they went to give their blood. Every day and every night after the accident, there were cops huddled outside the hospital, gathered by the bed-side, waiting nervously in the hallways, waiting for the test-results. Was there any blood flowing to the brain of their wounded comrade? Officer Ortiz's wife, herself an emer-gency-room nurse, vowed to wait until no blood was reach-ing her husband's brain. Three days after he was first wheeled in, she realized that there was virtually no hope for survival, and the unfathomable, painful decision was made to remove Officer Ortiz from life-support. Three hours later, Philadel-phia lost its first police officer since 1997.

It was 52 degrees as I headed north on the Roosevelt Bou-levard, my best friend in the passenger seat, and the rain that had been coming down for several days was showing no signs of letting up. I guess that was as it should have been. As we made the left turn onto Old Bustelton Avenue it was 9:40am, the viewing was not scheduled to start until 10:00, but hun-dreds of officers were already there. I rolled down my win-dow and the traffic policeman standing in the street in his long bright-yellow overcoat asked if I was, "friend or fam-ily?". I was technically neither but I realized that, today, I was both. After a beat I answered, "Friend", and I was directed to pull into the already-overflowing parking lot of Maternity BVM Church. The only free spot that I could find was next to a white, two-door Oldsmobile. On the rear window of that car, written in soap, were the words, "In Memory of My Cousin, Jose Ortiz". And so began what was to be my first police funeral.

My hands shook as we stood outside the church in a line of mourners that, within minutes, curved and snaked all along the block. I decided that my hands shook partly from the cold, but mostly due to the turmoil that was going on inside me, and around me. To my right, officers from many different towns, townships, cities and states began to file in. Some of their faces were somber, some of them were nervous, some of them were simply expressionless— except for their eyes. To my left, out-of-view, a relative of Jose Ortiz's was weeping and retching, shattered by the thought that today was ordained as the day that final good-byes must be said. Several relatives tried earnestly to calm the woman down and bring her into the church. Eventually she was sedate enough to enter, but a wheelchair was on-hand with an officer stationed behind it for the duration of the service, just in case she could not bring herself to walk any further.

After paying respects to Officer Ortiz's body, my friend and I sat in the fourth or fifth pew from the back, on the right side, leaving the entire left side of the church free for police officers. Of course, the left side of the church was not wholly sufficient, and officers spilled on into the right side, sitting in front of and behind me. Officers also stood all along the sides of the church, and at the rear. As they passed me after viewing Officer Ortiz's body, I saw their shoulder-patches. From Pennsylvania, officers from Abington, Allentown, Bensalem, Bristol, Bucks County, Cheltenham, Darby, Plymouth Township, and many others appeared to pay their respects. Also there were members of the Pennsylvania State Police, Amtrak Police Department, University of Pennsylvania Police Department and cadets from the Philadelphia Police Academy. Of course, 25th District officers were most, if not all present, as well hundreds of other Philadelphia police officers. Lawmen also poured in from New Jersey, their State Police were especially well-represented. A patrolman from the 60th Precinct of the New York City Police Department also came to pay his respects, as did as an officer from the United States Park Police. The Philadelphia Police Department brass, the Mayor, and other city dignitaries were also present. Behind us, as the viewing was drawing to a close, I could hear Officer Ortiz's sister kidding around with Ortiz's three year old daughter, Nicole. I marveled at the strength that it must have taken for Officer Ortiz's sister to mask her pain long enough to joke with a little girl, too young to fully understand that her father was gone. Ortiz's sister completed her joking just in time to help her relatives try and calm her sister-in-law as the coffin was closed forever.

While the family was having its final moment with Officer Ortiz, the organ stopped its mournful droning. Nobody spoke a word, for we were all aware of the sorrowful moment taking place at the other end of the church. The perfect silence was shattered by the lamentable wails of Officer Ortiz's widow. "You promised you'd always be with me!" she cried to her dead husband's body. She pleaded with him to take her with him but, as the casket was closed, she turned her cries to God, screaming, "God give me strength!" and then, with great courage, she asked the question that was on the minds of every human being sitting in that church, "Why?". At the asking of that unanswerable question, I am sure that I heard a thousand hearts all break at once.

Prayers were read by a family-member and Ortiz's partner and, after that, all Catholics in the church were invited to take part in Communion, the acceptance of the Eucharist. Then a speech was made by Officer Ortiz's sister, Noemi. She spoke of her brother's long-time wish to become a police officer, she called him her "guardian angel", and she thanked all of the mourners for their presence and their support. In the middle of her speech, as if in a movie, the drummers that were standing outside in the rain slowly began to play. It was a mistake, of course, somebody had possibly given the wrong command at the wrong time, but the drums got louder, their sharp, military rattling invading the church, and the words and thoughts of a broken sister. Within a few seconds, somebody outside must have realized that the drums were being played much too early. The drums ceased, but not before Officer Ortiz's sister, her voice breaking, said, "It's too much". I don't know if that was part of her speech, or if it was in response to the heightening raps of the drums, but whether she meant to or not, she captured the sentiments of that day for me just perfectly. It was, quite simply, too much.

As the speeches drew to a close I noted, somewhat unhappily and perplexingly, that not one word was spoken about Officer Tina Hudrick, the officer whose car had accidentally hit Officer Ortiz. I thought it was strange that, at a Catholic Mass, the mourners were not encouraged to pray for Officer Hudrick too. I felt sure that the Reverend would have gently asked the congregation to forgive the officer, to try and understand her feelings of pain and loss on this day. But nobody spoke of her, nobody mentioned her name that I heard, either in malice or in sympathy. In fact, I do not even know if she was in attendance at the funeral. Probably not, I surmised. After all, the last I heard she was still not back to work, on sedatives, not speaking to many people, and recovering from her own injuries. As the Reverend directed us to turn to our right or left and "offer each other some sign of peace", I found my thoughts turning to Officer Hudrick. I wanted to offer her peace— but she was not physically there with me that I knew of— and nobody bade me offer her peace. I had to do it in my heart, secretly, as if I were doing something wrong. I know that I was not doing something wrong, but it certainly felt that way at the moment. I am sorry that the people of this city, many times eager to point a finger after a tragedy, were not given encouragement by anyone to find it in their hearts to forgive and bid peace to Officer Tina Hudrick.

After a touching speech was made by Officer Ortiz's Captain, the directive that all uniformed officers exit and assemble outside the church was given. I watched them all leave, some reaching out for each others' arms, some digging their white gloves into their eyes, as if to somehow push their tears back inside their heads. One young police officer was unsuccessfully trying to choke back his sobs. He was right next to me, and I wanted to stand up and touch this man's shoulder. I wanted to tell him that there was no need for him to try and stop his tears— but I couldn't— all I could do was watch.

Pallbearers from the 25th District, the Ortiz family, and civilian mourners like myself were the only ones left in the church at this time. The pallbearers wheeled the casket to the forefront of the church and then, right before me, draped the sliver coffin with the American flag, tucking it securely beneath the casket-handles. Then, from outside, the mournful, haunting bagpipes geared up and began to cry. Jose Ortiz's mother too began to cry and, as the cameras whirred and clicked outside, it seemed to me as if this day would never end. Between the bagpipes outside and Officer Ortiz's mother inside and the church's organ, all going at once, my head was spinning to the point where I needed to grab onto the pew in front of me for support. As if the weeping of the pipes and the mother were not enough, the Heavens were also in this competition, throwing down their frigid tears, blowing them without compassion, into the faces of all the mourners.

The parking lot and adjacent streets at this point took on a sound that I found incongruous, considering the present scene. Suddenly the air was filled with the sounds of engines, all 8 cylinder, firing up. For a moment, I thought that I was at the Indianapolis Motor Speedway, awaiting the start of the 500. Hundreds of police cars, vans, trucks, sport utility vehicles, and motorcycles all started up, one right after the other, in preparation for the long, winding journey to Holy Sepulcher Cemetery. As my friend and I walked towards my car, many officers inside the parking lot and on the street turned on their sirens. This produced a cacophony of yelps, wails, and screams, creating an air of uncertainty and chaos— a scene probably like the one played out on Cambria Street, on the day that Officer Ortiz fell.

It was still raining as we all got on the road together. Civilian and unmarked police vehicles were assigned to file out first and, on a long stretch of road, I could see, very far behind me, the blurry dancing lights of the police motorcade. Thankfully, all sirens were turned off during the procession. All along the route police cruisers were parked at every intersection, two south-bound lanes of the Roosevelt Boulevard were closed off so that our cortege could proceed. Some of the officers standing by their cruisers saluted the procession, some just stood in the rain and watched. The rain had let up somewhat and I opened my window to get some air. On the other side of one street, where traffic was blocked up completely, someone in a red Chevrolet Blazer attempted to get out of the jam by making an illegal U-turn into the procession. An officer standing nearby on traffic duty saw this, stormed up to the driver and screamed, "Hey! You get back in there!". The driver of the Blazer obeyed. There was no room for impatience today, no room for disrespect. For the people in that procession, and for the officers protecting it outside, today was sacred.

It took us approximately one hour to get from the church to the cemetery, at a more-or-less steady rate of 40-45 miles per hour. Once we got out of the car, the rain bore down with a fierceness it had not shown us yet today. The sky was simply not ready to make known the full force of its sorrow. But it had restrained itself long enough, and it would not hold in its grief any longer. It could not have picked a more appropriate time to begin the downpour.

My friend and I stood on the sopping wet grass, facing the bereaved family and various police dignitaries who were huddled together under their dark green canopy. The Philadelphia Police Department Honor Guard stood at the ready, next to Officer Ortiz's family. Behind them, rows of Philadelphia police officers, about a dozen deep, stood as well. The bagpipers, drummers, bugler, and riflemen all stood on the other side of the family. Lines of police officers from other departments, stood on the sloping ground next to us, waiting. We waited too, and a young man from the funeral home handed each of us a flower. The biting-cold wind and rain battered us all, and I clenched my jaw just to stop it from trembling. The pallbearers assembled by the back-door of the hearse, which finally opened after a tormenting wait. The casket was brought out, and the order was given for all officers to salute.

The 26th of September, 2000 was a struggle for everybody who was present at Holy Sepulcher Cemetery. For the pallbearers, it was a struggle to keep their emotions from interfering with their delicate and painful duties. For all of the officers present, it was a struggle to look strong and supportive. For the Ortiz family, it was a struggle to figure out what they could possibly have done to deserve all this suffering. For me, it was a struggle to figure out whether the drenching amounts of wetness on my face were tears or rain. However, I think it is safe to say that nobody struggled more than the bagpipers at that cemetery, playing as Officer Ortiz's casket was brought out of the hearse. I mean absolutely no disrespect to those men, because I am confident that they are excellent musicians— but it was unmistakable, even to my musically untrained ear, that those bagpipes faltered. Maybe it was the rain, maybe it was something to do with the instruments themselves, or maybe it was something else. It has been a long time since those instruments have been played at a policeman's funeral. I thought to myself that maybe the lips that pursed against those rosewood pipes were just as unprepared for today as I was.

Family-members and friends gathered around the canopy, and it was impossible to see what I knew was occurring. The prayer was being said, the flag was being folded, and it was given to Officer Ortiz's widow, Theresa. It all happened so quietly that, when the first shot of the rifle salute rang out, I was startled momentarily, and my head sprang up. Two more shots were fired, to honor the dead policeman. Taps was played and, for the first time in Philadelphia Police Department history, two police helicopters roared above our heads. They flew side-by-side until they approached the site of mourning below. While one helicopter flew straight, the other one broke away in "missing man formation", to signal that Officer Ortiz had now departed from his job, his family, and his mortal life. The bagpipes, now strong and sure, blared out "Amazing Grace". Upon completion of the sad, piercing song, the order was barked out for us to disperse. After we placed our flowers on the casket, that is what we did. Two hours later, the sun was out.

Ten hours after the fact, I can hear everything and, if I close my eyes, I can see everything. I know that, ten years from now I will still be able to hear and see everything. There are certain events that occur in a person's life that time just cannot erase. I am certain and thankful that the funeral for 25th District Philadelphia Police Officer Jose Manuel Ortiz is one of those events for me. Although I was a civilian, not technically a citizen of Philadelphia, and not a family member or friend of Officer Ortiz, being there felt very right to me. After five long years of law enforcement activism, and many more ahead of me, I was finally where I belonged— I was finally amongst the throng.

Civilian Back-Up

{and other crazy ideas}

"Any jackass can break down a door, but it takes a skilled carpenter to build one."
— **Sam Rayburn;** *former Speaker of the House.*

Tragically, the murderous, the insane, the desperate, and the cowardly will continue to kill police officers in America— as long as there are cops, there will be cop-killers. But while violent men and women walk the streets with weapons, just looking to center their sights on a shiny badge, we must tirelessly make it harder for them to pull the trigger. It is up to us, the thinking, feeling, caring masses to put the squeeze on the insidiously dangerous minority that slays our police officers. We cannot depend upon politicians to do it, because they do not have the time to devote to this issue, nor do many of them have the interest. We cannot depend upon police departments to do it, because they have us to protect. We, on the other hand, have no one to protect, but our protectors.

Perhaps some of you may feel that it is not your responsibility, your obligation to help, I am of the opinion that it is. Why shouldn't we take some responsibility for assisting those who watch over us while we sleep? Isn't it only fair that we should give something back? True, it is quite easy to point fingers and assign blame when the police do something wrong but, as Sam Rayburn pointed out, "Any jackass can break down a door, but it takes a skilled carpenter to build one",

My second visit to the National Law Enforcement Officers Memorial. David M. Basner, photographer. 25 May, 1999

just as it takes a "skilled carpenter", not a "jackass" to care enough to want to solve a problem. And, no, the $25.00 you donate to your local FOP Lodge is not what I am referring to. It is a great start, though. What I am proposing has less to do with money than it has to do with activism. When most people hear the word "activism", they undoubtedly conjure up images of bra-burning, Civil-Rights marches, and anti-war demonstrations. Well, this is a different type of activism, but I don't believe that it is any less effective.

I have said that we cannot rely on politicians to create safer environments for police officers. I apologize, because that statement was somewhat misleading. What I meant to say was, we cannot rely on politicians to think of things on their own to protect police officers. We most certainly can give them a little nudge in the right direction, though. Through writing letters to congressmen, senators, governors and mayors, our ideas can actually become law. While these letters are not commonly read by the actual official, they are all read and forwarded to appropriate personnel and good ideas are always taken seriously. There are currently bills floating around the Senate and House that benefit police officers right now. One bill, HR 2710 would create a full-scale museum in Washington, DC at the site of the National Law Enforcement Officers Memorial. Another example of a bill that has been proposed is the possibility of legislation mandating bullet-proof front windshields in police cruisers. This is a very posi-tive first start, however, this bill has problems. Bulletproof front windshields will do very little to save the lives of police officers who are killed by suspects shooting through the side and rear windows. Also, the cost of these beefed-up cruisers will probably be too much for smaller departments to handle. Lastly, used police vehicles are often sold to the general pub-lic after they are retired from police service. I shudder to think about the crimes that will be committed by suspects driving ex-police cars with bulletproof front windshields as getway cars. Those suspects will be pretty hard to stop if the situa-tion comes down to gunplay.

Perhaps a better way to decrease the number of police officers killed in the line of duty is to provide every law en-forcement officer in America with a bulletproof vest. Shock-ingly, there are police departments that simply cannot afford vests and, consequently, officers are shot and killed in the streets due to lack of proper funds. It is true, bulletproof vests are not the cure-all panacea that they appear to be. There are certain types of bullets that can easily penetrate body armor. Also, the officer's sides are not covered by the vest and, if the officer is shot in the side and the bullet travels at a certain angle, it can easily pierce the officer's heart. And, of course, not all police officers who wear their vests are shot in the chest. Because of the abundance of body armor, many people who kill police officers will not even bother with a body shot, they will simply aim for the head. Waterbury Connecticut Police Officer Walter Williams was having a conversation with a suspect when the suspect "accidentally" bumped into the officer, putting his hands on the officer's chest to regain his balance. It was no accident— the suspect put his hands against Officer Williams' chest to feel for a vest. Indeed, Officer Williams was wearing his vest that day, and so the suspect shot him in the face.

Body armor is not perfect, but it does save lives. On the seventh of January, 1999, in Philadelphia, undercover narcotics officer Alfred Diggs was shot once in the chest. Fortunately he was wearing his vest. Without it, the shot probably would have killed him. He was taken to Temple University Hospital and, much to the surprise and relief of his family, was released the very same day. It is because of cases like Alfred Diggs' and many others, that federally-appropriated money should be made available to ensure that every single police department has enough money to purchase vests for their officers. Additionally, money should be made available in the form of research grants for companies who manufacture bulletproof vests. This money should be used to create vests that are lightweight, but are still capable of stopping most bullets, and these vests should be more comfortable for officers to wear all day, especially during hot weather. Because bulletproof vests are so heavy, many officers cannot bear to wear them through an entire shift. The officers, literally drenched in sweat, will sometimes remove their vests due to the fact that it is just too oppressively hot underneath, and so officers die because they are hot. Once better, more qualitative vests are commonplace, their use by officers should be absolutely mandatory, and any officer caught by a supervisor without one should be reprimanded and fined— after all, it is for their own protection. Vest technology will continue to progress and evolve, and, thankfully, bulletproof vests will continue to take hits intended for hearts.

As illustrated earlier, traffic-stops are very dangerous situations for police officers. According to the National Law Enforcement Officers Memorial statistics, to this date, approximately 300 police officers have been killed during traffic stops, and around 240 of those officers were shot to death. If the vehicle the officer is stopping has a very dirty license plate, or no license plate at all, the officer will have no information about the driver he is about to rendezvous with. He is truly flying blind. Many police departments in America deploy one-man cars, a single officer patrolling the streets in a squad car alone. The decision to do this usually has to do with the geographic make-up of the patrol-sector, the financial situation of the department, or public opinion. Some citizens get annoyed when they see a two-man car because some people are of the opinion that, if the officer were in another car, there would be more police out on the street, which, technically is true. However, most people who complain about "ineffective patrol management" fail to take officer safety into consideration. It is simply much safer for a police officer to be riding on patrol with another officer, it is instant back-up. It would eliminate situations where a motorist is alone with a police officer and, if an incident occurs, it is the motorist's word against the policeman's. A police officer might be less inclined to act inappropriately if another officer, possibly of higher rank, is present. Sadly, even officers in two-man cars are killed. Dallas Police Officer Robert Wood, cited in a previous chapter, was the lead officer in a two-man car the night he was murdered. In a two-man car, the lead officer approaches the driver's side of the suspect vehicle, while the other officer stands at the rear, watching for suspicious movements or behavior inside the car. After Wood was shot, his partner, one of the first female officers in Texas to be assigned to radio-car patrol duty, emptied her revolver in the direction of the fleeing vehicle.

Despite the fact that officers in two-man cars are killed, the fact remains that having two officers in any given situation is better than having one. Many times, and officer will find himself outnumbered on a traffic-stop and back-up isn't always right around the corner. On the 23rd of January, 1991, the Nacogdoches County, Texas Sheriff's Department lost a veteran officer in such a circumstance. Constable Darrell Lunsford was patrolling in a one-man unit when he stopped a vehicle, containing three men, on suspicion of narcotics-trafficking. Constable Lunsford's hunch proved to be correct, marijuana was found in the car. As Lunsford moved in to make the arrest, he was attacked by the suspects. They wrestled and rolled about on the shoulder of the highway for what seemed like forever. Car after car, their drivers oblivious to the murder that was about to take place on the side of the road, passed right on by that night. Despite the fact that Constable Lunsford was an experienced, tough man, he was no match for the three determined suspects who finally got control of Lunsford's gun after a ferocious struggle, and shot him with it. There was no back-up officer to help Lunsford fight off his attackers that night. There was no one there to fire at the fleeing vehicle, or to perform CPR on the dying officer. The only other eyes watching that horrible night were the "eyes" of the small video camera, mounted atop the dashboard in Darrell Lunsford's police cruiser. Several years later, thousands of people watching "20/20" saw the whole thing as the tape was broadcast on the show and, like the video camera, they could do nothing to stop it. I was one of the people who sat watching, riveted to the television screen. I watched Darrell Lunsford die. I too could do nothing to stop it, and it broke my heart. After viewing this, and other horrifying incidents, it has become quite clear to me that it is safer for the police officer, and the citizen, to have two-man cars wherever and whenever possible.

Reading the previous section, it may apear that I am criticizing the use of dash-mounted cameras. Nothing could be further from the truth. That video camera does an infinite amount to help an officer in trouble— in a manner of speaking. When a police officer makes a traffic stop, the camera records the exact car that has been stopped, its license plate and, if the suspect gets out of the vehicle, it records all of his features. If the suspect speaks, it records his voice. If the suspect kills, it records the killing. Even if an officer dies in a hail of gunfire and the suspect gets away before back-up can arrive, that tape will be studied and, many times, it will point the officers directly to the killers. Also, it must be rather devastating for a defense-attorney to sit in a courtroom and watch his client kill a police officer, on television. However, as unarguably helpful as the video camera is in catching and prosecuting a suspect, it is totally ineffective with regards to saving an officer's life.

While we are on the subject of traffic stops, there is one last area which speaks to officer protection that I must explore. I will say it plain, tinted windows frighten me, even as a citizen, they frighten me. It is just a weird feeling, pulling up next to a car and— while they can see you just fine— you can hardly see them at all. If I were a police officer stopping a car with tinted windows, I am sure that it would scare the hell out of me. Usually, when a police officer stops a motorist, even if dispatch is unable to provide any information about the subject in the car, the officer can basically make out the suspect. Also he can see, more-or-less, what the suspect is doing inside the car through the back window before he even approaches the car. However, if the vehicle the officer has stopped has tinted windows, not only can the officer not report to dispatch an approximate description of the suspect, he can't even see what the suspect is doing inside the car, or even how many people are in the car. The suspect, or suspects, could be loading up a machine gun and pointing it right at the officer who, ambling on up to the driver's window, would never even know it. Let us be honest, shall we? There is absolutely no practical reason why anyone would need tinted windows. They are not a necessity, they are a luxury, and a questionable one at that. It is my opinion that severely-tinted windows, ones so dark that you cannot see the occupant inside, and mirror-tinted windows are a serious detriment to officer-safety, and should be banned. The driver of any car with tinted windows should be given a fair amount of time to get the windows changed, and, after that, if the owner of the vehicle still refuses to comply, his car should be impounded. Officers have enough trouble on traffic stops without being able to see the motorist inside the car they just pulled over. Of course, not all officers who are killed in the line of duty die as a result of dangerous felons. Sometimes policemen die for other reasons, equally as shameful, if not more so.

It amazes me to see how negligent and just plain stupid certain police departments can be sometimes. Purchasing agents are responsible for buying equipment, ranging from guns to radios to cars for police officers in their department. It is not only the purchasing agent's responsibility to get the most cost-effective equipment, it is his or her responsibility to get equipment that is not going to fail under the rigors of police work. What does the purchasing agent have to do with officer safety? Plenty. Faulty equipment can kill police officers too.

The former Commissioner of the New York City Police Department, Patrick V. Murphy has been quoted as saying that, "Patrol is the backbone of policing". If that is true, then it can be said that, in the modern age, the patrol car is the backbone of patrol. The patrol car enables an officer to move freely about the streets, alleys, and freeways that comprise his beat. Without his car, the police officer is incapable of a rapid response to an emergency, nor can he chase a fleeing motorist. The vast majority of officers in America probably spend more time in their patrol cars than they do in their own beds. They eat meals in their cars, drink ridiculous amounts of coffee in their cars, and they complete an abundance of paperwork in their cars. This car, this police vehicle, must be capable of astounding feats. It must possess mercuric acceleration and superior stopping abilities. Additionally, it must be large enough inside to accommodate bulky radio, radar, and siren equipment, a shotgun, a safety-cage, at least one, many times too large officers wearing uncomfortable duty-belts, and one-or-more prisoners in the back. However, it must also be something else. The police car must— it absolutely must— be safe.

Every year, the Michigan State Police tests "police package" vehicles proffered by various auto manufacturers, to see which of these vehicles would be best suited for patrol duties. Each vehicle tested by the Michigan State Police is rated for acceleration, braking, interior ergonomics, and fuel economy. The vehicles are not crash-tested. Apparently, police cars are held up to the same stringent safety standards that civilian cars are held to, but one wonders whether purchasing agents for police departments pay attention to the safety of the vehicles they are buying for young men and women that they have probably never even met. It is my assumption that most purchasing agents are really concerned with how fast these cars can move, how many miles they get to each gallon of gas, and which car is the cheapest to buy and maintain. While this isn't necessarily wrong, not at all, the safety of the police officer inside that car must also be considered. Many police officers die each year while in their cars. According to statistics gathered by the Officer Down Memorial Page, (www.odmp.org), 46 police officers died in their police vehicles in 1999, 52 in 1998, and 48 in 1997. This is tragic, but, keeping in mind that police officers spend most of their shifts in their cars, (sometimes during fast responses and/or dangerous pursuits), it is understandable. What is harder to understand is how some police departments, in good conscience, buy police vehicles for officers when the safety of the cars they are buying is dubious at best. The prime example that I can think of is the 1990 Chevrolet Caprice.

Historically, Chrysler dominated the police car market with such popular cars as the Plymouth Belvedere, Dodge Polara, and the Plymouth Fury, and its sister car, the Dodge Monaco. However, when Chrysler bowed out of the police car game in 1989, after its decision not to produce the successful Plymouth Gran Fury and Dodge Diplomat anymore, police departments across America were essentially left with two choices— the 1990 Ford Crown Victoria and the 1990 Chevrolet Caprice. Many departments opted for the 1990 Chevrolet Caprice. It was big, fast, comfortable, and, for a car without anti-lock brakes, it stopped rather well. Then again, the 1990 Ford Crown Victoria was also big, fast, comfortable, and, for a car without anti-lock brakes, it stopped rather well too. The 1990 Crown Vic. also had a driver's side airbag, and the Caprice did not. But purchasing agents all have their favorites, and, for many reasons, the Caprice won many a bid that year. The 1990 Chevrolet Caprice did have one interesting "safety-feature" that the Crown Victoria did not have—the Caprice had a passive restraint system called the "door mounted safety harness". Basically, all this was comprised of was an ordinary seat belt but, instead of it being mounted on the B-pillar of the car, it was mounted on the door, and most people probably never even noticed the difference at first. As time progressed, many problems quickly arose with this particular safety-belt design and the National Highway Transportation Safety Administration received numerous complaints, many of them from police departments. Some of the complaints stated that the seat belt "obstructs vision when looking left", and that it "cuts across neck & face," (NHTSA; ODI ID: 367755). Also, more than one police department reported that the seat belt "catches on uniform gear when exiting in hurry," (NHTSA; ODI ID: 375647). But that is not the worst of it. Three reports were filed to the NHTSA when a police officer in New England was killed in his 1990 Chevrolet Caprice. The driver's side door opened during the collision and the seat belt, which was mounted on the door, was rendered totally ineffective. NHTSA incident complaint reports 371265, 375434, and 375660 all concern the police fatality due almost entirely to the failure of the door-mounted seat belt on the 1990 Chevrolet Caprice.

Many police departments were unsatisfied with the design of the seat belt and had expressed concerns about possible police fatalities resulting from ejection even before the New England officer died. Just looking at the belt's design, which was wisely re-designed for the 1991 model year, raises serious questions about the belt's ability to secure the driver in the event of a crash serious enough to force the door open. Why any police department would have chosen this car over the comparable Crown Victoria, which did not have this dangerous seat belt design and did have a driver's side airbag, is simply beyond me.

In addition to purchasing safe, reliable equipment for police officers, it is up to police departments and supervisors to make sure that every police officer who leaves the police building has everything that he or she needs to perform the duties of a police officer. No police officer would be sent out on patrol without his gun, or his pants, correct? This would all appear to be common sense, would it not? However, police officers are somtimes incongruously sent out on patrol without certain things that are essential. Radios, for example, are unquestionably necessary for every police officer in the world. Without a radio, how does an officer call dispatch with a request, either for a routine question, or for assistance in an emergency situation? What is he supposed to do— use smoke-signals?

A friend of mine recently attended a concert at Veteran's Stadium in Philadelphia, Pennsylvania and the parking lot was patrolled by Philadelphia police officers. My friend had just been scammed by someone in the parking lot, and he approached a uniformed officer to ask for help. The suspect was clearly visible in the parking lot and my friend identified him to the officer, and told him what had occurred. The officer proceeded to walk towards the suspect, and the suspect began to walk away— then he took off running. The police officer did not pursue. When my friend asked why the officer did not chase and apprehend the fleeing suspect, the officer replied apologetically that he was reluctant to get involved in a foot pursuit because he did not have a radio on him and he could not broadcast his changing location to dispatch.

I could not believe what I was hearing as my friend related this story to me several days later. The fact that any department, especially a big-city department, would dare send any officer out on patrol without a police radio confuses and enrages me. What if the suspect that officer was strolling towards so casually turned around and just decided to shoot that officer? If that officer had been properly equipped with a radio, he could have used it to call for assistance or, if he was unconcious or dead, a passerby could have used it for that purpose, to get help. Police officers need radios, and, more importantly, they need radios that work. Police officers need big, strong, fast, safe police cars, I am sorry, but there are too many officers dying each year in their patrol cars, and there are too many thoughtless people purchasing those cars on a whim. And, most importantly, every law enforcement officer in this country needs an effective, comfortable bulletproof vest. It should not even be an issue. If a department cannot afford vests for its officers and the government does not adequately step in, that department should be holding carwashes, or bake sales if necessary. The price of a vest might be high, but the price of an officer's blood is infinitely higher.

We all know that guns kill many police officers each year. Automobiles, whether they be police cars or civilian vehicles, also cause a great amount of law enforcement deaths. However, there is a much less talked about killer stalking this nation's police officers, remorselessly striking down a surprisingly high amount of officers. This killer is called the heart attack, and it is just as deadly as any homicidal assassin. Due to the high-stress nature of police work, law enforcement officers are very susceptible to heart attacks, and, many times, they occur when the officer is on duty. According to the Officer Down Memorial webpage, (www.odmp.org), from 1995-2000, eighty six police officers in this country died as a result of a line-of-duty heart attack. In 1999, there were 144 law enforcement fatalities, and heart attacks ranked as the third highest killer of police officers that year. It is becoming increasingly evident that every police officer should have a portable defibrillator with him, in his police car, at all times. Obviously, officers would have to be rigorously trained in the machine's use before this policy could be implemented, but every police car in America should eventually be equipped with this life-saving device. That way, if a police officer collapses, say, in the department parking lot, or at the scene of a traffic-stop, there will be no need to waste precious seconds while waiting for an ambulance. Although all police officers are trained in basic CPR, rapid access to a defibrillator machine could potentially save the lives of many stricken police officers. In addition to that, police officers having defibrillators with them would be of great benefit to civilians because many times the police are the first ones to arrive at the scene of a civilian cardiac case. With the startling statistic of 86 dead peace officers in five years, all killed by their own hearts, it is evident that funding needs to be made available for departments to purchase defibrillators for their police officers, in order to save their own lives.

There is something else that I believe can be done to benefit police officers in America. It is not something that purchasing agents can do, it is not even something that police chiefs can do. This one's for us. Every time a police officer is felled in America, a silent emergency call goes out. That call does not reach the ear of a police dispatcher, it does not reach the local rescue ambulance squad— that call is directed at the hearts of every American man, woman, and child. It is a call that is quite similar to the actual call that goes out when a policeman has just been killed, "Officer down! Assist the officer!". Well we, as citizens, can't just jump in our cars every time a police officer has been gunned down and race to the scene, but we can provide our own form of assistance. I like to call this type of assistance, "Civilian Back-Up", if you will.

Civilian Back-Up is not so much something that we can do to prevent the murders of policemen, but it is something that we can do to show that we recognize the tragedy, that we too mourn the passing of police officers. It is something we can do to show our support for police officers, both living and dead, that we support police wives and police widows. It is something we can do to show that we are outraged at the killing, and the killer. It is something we can do to show that we want justice. We can do the "small" things that carry the big impact.

Wear a pin. If you go to the National Law Enforcement Officer's Memorial in Washington, DC, (a beautiful, heart-breaking place that every American citizen should visit at least once in their life), you can purchase a beautiful lapel pin for a very reasonable price. Also, proceeds from the sale get pumped right back into the Memorial. Wear the pin proudly, wear it every day. I wear mine proudly, every day. People will come up to you and ask you what it is, what it represents. There is very little in life that I enjoy more than when some-body comes up to me to ask me about my pins. It is a wonder-ful, small way to "inform and educate". They may ask you stupid questions like "Is that a boyscout pin?" or "Oh, that's a cricket medal, right?", and, my personal favorite, "Why are you wearing a pin for the Pennsylvania Turnpike?", (the de-sign of the pin is a deep blue badge with a rose across it. The badge, remotely, resembles the insignia for the PA Turnpike). Enlighten your interrogators, tell them what that pin stands for. Let them know that over 15,000 police officers have died in the line of duty in this country since 1792. Don't be afraid to tell the world, because the world doesn't know. If a police officer in your town or city dies and you hear about it, put a small strip of black tape across the center of that pin. Tie a deep blue ribbon, (the color for law enforcement support), around your car's antenna or rear-view mirror to show your support and your grief.

Something else we can do for slain police officers is turn up the heat on cop-killers who are on the run. Watch the news when special reports concerning a fleeing cop-killer are broadcast in your area. Pay extra attention, and keep your eyes and ears open everywhere you go. If you happen to live in New York, there is an even better way. COP-SHOT, (Citizens Outraged at Police Being Shot), is an organization that was founded by civilians several years ago to actively get citizens involved in hunting down cop-killers. If you look on the bumper of any NYPD radio car, you will undoubtedly see a "1 -800-COP-SHOT" bumper-sticker. The 1-800 refers to an anonymous tip-line set up by COP-SHOT where anybody, even convicted felons, who has information regarding the wounding or killing of a New York City patrolman can call in with. If the information leads to a conviction, the caller will be the recipient of $10,000—no questions asked. Although COP-SHOT is of tremendous benefit to New York City, the organization receives no government funding whatsoever, they rely strictly on private donations to keep in operation. I am sure a donation would be greatly appreciated, not just by COP-SHOT, but by 41,000 New York City patrolmen. This is one way to help but, of course, there are others.

If you can, and it's not too far away, go to an officer's funeral. Bring a friend. Better yet, if you are married and have children, take your husband or wife and take your children. Respect for law enforcement does not just happen, it is taught, just as respect for anything is taught. Take your child to your local police department's open house. Let him or her talk to police officers— they're just people, most of them with children of their own. I think, as a child, my parents never took me to our police department because they were scared. Believe me, there is nothing to be scared of, I am sure they would love to have you and your child over for a bit. For the most part, because officers and civilians are separated from each other until there is a big problem, officers sometimes do not know what to make of civilians, and definitely vice-versa. That is a shame.

One of the nicest half-hours I ever passed in my life was on a bench outside a small police department near my house. At that time I was looking to buy an ex-police car, a 1990 Ford Crown Victoria, (no door-mounted safety belts for me), and, at that time, this particular department had a whole fleet of those cars still in-service. My father and I went to the department and came upon an older police officer, (a dead-ringer for the actor Robert Duvall), sitting on a bench, eating his lunch, and we apologized for interrupting him. Not only did he invite us to sit down with him, he spoke freely and honestly about the pros and cons of owning an ex-police cruiser, specifically the 1990 Crown Vic. He was kind, informative, helpful, and courteous. At the end of our conversation, he remarked that he was preparing to retire to South Carolina, I believe. I thought to myself that the retirement of Officer Francis Gagliardi was the loss of the Haverford Township, Pennsylvania Police Department, and the citizens of that township. I promised myself that I would not forget the time we spent talking that gorgeous spring day, the brilliant sun spilling down on us. I didn't forget. A year later, I called on Officer Gagliardi, (who was still working despite his retirement plans), again to ask if I could interview him for a project I was doing for my high-school English class. He agreed. I interviewed Officer Gagliardi on the telephone, this time for about two hours, and I got an "A" on the project, in no small part due to the efforts and the generosity of Officer Francis Gagliardi. Thinking of any way I could possibly thank him, I composed a letter of genuine thanks and commendation to the Haverford Township Police Department about Officer Gagliardi, which, I was assured, was placed in his permanent file. Despite the fact that officers in and around the area where I live are accessible and eager to have civilian contact, and despite the fact that a police officer lives just down the street from my old house, that time on the park-bench with Officer Gagliardi was the first time I had ever spoken to a policeman in my life. I was sixteen years old.

Police officers are strange creatures. When they are in need of help, they will almost exclusively call upon, and rely on other police officers. The fact that there are civilians out there who are willing to provide assistance and support is an idea that is unfamiliar to most police officers in the United States. Let's get them more familiar with that idea. Write letters. Write letters of sympathy to an officer's family when an officer is killed, send a get-well card to the hospital if an officer is shot or otherwise injured. Toss off a quick email to a recently bereaved police department, they will appreciate your words more than you could ever know. Write letters of anger to newspapers and politicians when you see people supporting a cop-killer instead of a cop. Write letters to parole boards when you read that a convicted cop-killer is becoming eligible for parole— write to deny the parole. People will listen, you just have to give them something to listen to. Write, write, write, write, write. As a citizen, I have come to reluctantly accept the fact that a police officer will probably never ask me for help, and he will probably never ask you either. But, then again, you also have to know that it is your obligation to bend down and offer assistance, even when it has not been requested, for that is usually when it is needed the most.

Two Allentown, Pennsylvania Police Officers. Jedediah Baker, photographer.

Flowers and Mourners

"IT'S AGAINST THE LAW TO SHOOT, IT'S AGAINST THE LAW TO MISS."

— Woody Guthrie

Policing is not the most dangerous job in the world, I freely acknowledge that fact, and I do not what you to think that I am trying to convince you that this is the case. Bearing that in mind, I would say that policing is the most difficult job in the world. Obviously, this is impossible to quantify, and that is why it is an opinion, not a fact. There are many Americans who support police officers, and there are many Americans who criticize, deride, and curse police officers. Most of the time, the people in the latter group do not even know why they are doing so. Every time a suspect is shot down by a police officer, these critics are at their most vociferous. However, when it is the police officer who is shot down by the suspect, these critics will say that it was the officer's own fault, that he should have fired first, or that a police officer's death simply "goes with the territory" of their job. Or, many times they will simply say nothing at all, because they just don't care.

The police officer in America is forever damned. He is destined to be unloved and unappreciated by many of the people he has sworn unconditionally to protect. He will be poked fun at by children who don't know any better, and he will be shot at by adults who also don't know any better. Usually, the only time the work, dedication, and the suffering of a police officer is acknowledged by the public will be after the officer has been slain by some pathetic coward. Even then, after the glorious and beautiful funeral, all is quickly forgotten, and the widow and her children are, once again, alone. All in all, I think that a great number of people in this country rise to judge police officers too quickly, most of the time before all of the facts are in. I believe that this happened recently when four police officers came upon a young man standing in a doorway, barely visible in the dark of a New York City night.

We all know the name of the victim: Amadou Diallo. We all know the number: 41 shots. Most of us know the names of the officers: Edward McMellon, Sean Carroll, Kenneth Boss, and Richard Murphy. The simple fact that an unarmed man died that night is horrible, it is a tragedy. What is also tragic is that, by and large, these officers were judged by many of the people of New York, but also by many people all over the world. People are angry, and rightfully so. When I heard about the shooting, after I had read about it in the New York Times, New York Daily News, and the Village Voice, I was angry too— I still am. I am angry that Amadou Diallo did not get his hands up in the air when he was ordered to do so, because then he would still be alive today. I know that people are furious over this case. However, one must struggle not to get so wrapped up in the Diallo family's pain that they can't step into the shoes of the four officers who were on patrol that night, looking for a serial rapist that allegedly fit Diallo's description. Can you imagine it?

Two of the officers approach the shadowy figure and ask him to show them his hands. Instead of doing so, he tries to open the door he is standing in front of. The order is given again, this time louder. The suspect does not comply. His hands disappear from view. The next thing an officer usually sees at this point is the barrel of a gun and the flash coming from the muzzle as the trigger is pulled. Diallo runs inside the building, tugging at something in his pocket. I ask you, honestly, what were they supposed to have done? Pressed "pause" and analyze the tape? Should they have asked, "Oh, excuse me, there, sir, but what's that thing you're going to pull out of your pocket to show me? Is that a gun? A wallet? What is that?". No, there simply isn't time. When a suspect refuses to comply with an officer's order to "show hands", the officer can no longer be responsible for what happens after that refusal to comply. I say that because the next series of events, (usually ending up with the suspect getting shot), have been decided, not by the officer, but the suspect. Many have speculated that there was some kind of language barrier that affected Diallo's ability to understand the officers' commands to show his hands. Diallo's roommates have stated that Diallo "spoke English well", according to a Court TV online article.

When the pivotal moment came and Officer Sean Carroll saw what he thought was a weapon, he cried, "Gun!", to alert his partner to the threat, and both officers began shooting. During the first few shots, fired by Officers Carroll and McMellon, McMellon, stepping backwards, fell off the vestibule steps, breaking his tailbone. Officer Carroll and the other two officers thought that McMellon had been shot by Diallo, so they all opened fire. When these circumstances were presented before a jury, the jury came to the same conclusion that I came to, that Amadou Diallo, through his own actions, was the cause of this terrible death, not the New York City patrolmen who fired the shots that night.

Many people, including the Reverend Al Sharpton, a vocal critic of anything in blue, have chosen to paint these officers as assassins, vicious animals who were just looking to kill a black man that night. They are seen by many as comparable to Klu Klux Klan members, and the tragic accident that took Amadou Diallo's life is compared to a premeditated lynching. What Reverend Sharpton and his acolytes fail to recognize is that these officers feared for their lives that night, as well as the lives of all of the people inside the building that Amadou Diallo fled into. I believe that those officers were terrified that night. The mere fact that only 19 out of 41 shots fired at Diallo actually struck him should tell you something about the officers' emotional state that night. A methodical killer would have a much higher degree of accuracy. A scared young police officer, with a heart and a conscience, misses like that. Those officers did their job that night, they identified themselves properly as police officers and requested, repeatedly, that the suspect show them his hands. It was Amadou Diallo who, as a resident in this country, failed to do his job.

Of course, it does not really matter what I think or feel, nor does it matter what Al Sharpton thinks or feels either. What matters is that, after twenty three hours of deliberation, a multi-racial jury unanimously exonerated each officer. All I am asking is that you deliberate, (perhaps not quite as dutifully as that jury did), before you form an opinion on a matter so weighty as a police officer's guilt or innocence. The decision to shoot a suspect is not a decision that any police officer makes in a cavalier manner, and the repercussions of that action will follow the officer all throughout his professional career, as well as his life. Just be judicious and careful before you pass judgment on the man or woman who has to make that split-second decision. Believe me, the officer who kills a suspect will probably judge himself harder than any police-critic ever could.

Lastly on this subject, for anybody who will say that the NYC officers should not have fired because they outnumbered Diallo, that there is no possible way that one or two suspects can defeat four police officers, it is with a heavy heart that I remind these critics of the "Newhall Incident". On the 6th of April, 1970, the veins of the California Highway Patrol were literally and figuratively torn open by two brutal assailants, Bobby Davis and Jack Twinning. The two men were stopped because Twinning and Davis were suspected of brandishing a weapon earlier in the day. Together, they killed California Highway Patrolmen Walter C. Frago, Roger D. Gore, James E. Pence, Jr. and George M. Alleyn— all were cut down ruthlessly in a four minute bloodbath. Pence and Alleyn were 24, Frago and Gore were 23.

I would also cite the far more recent case of suspect Arthur Alalouf, who downed four NYC cops in one horrible event. It was August 12th, 2000 when Mr. Alalouf's parents went to their local precinct house to inform officers that their son had threatened them. They also told the desk officer that, if police responded to Alalouf's house, that Alalouf would shoot them on sight. Alalouf proved as good as his word. In the ensuing madness, Officer Gregory John, (the first downed officer), was shot in the shoulder. Bronx E.S.U. Officer Jose Guerra was shot in the face and leg. Officer William Fischer was shot by Alalouf in the leg. Police finally shot and killed Alalouf after he had shot Officer Joseph Ocasio with a shotgun. A frightening example of four officers, easily outnumbered and out-gunned by one assailant.

While serious amounts of faultfinding are directed at police officers day in and day out in this society courtesy of the American citizenry, there is a darker, more disturbing source of critique that police officers must deal with when a questionable action committed in the line of duty occurs. Police officers must continually answer to other police officers.

Los Angeles Police Department plainclothes Officers Ian Campbell and Karl Hettinger had only been partners for several days, but were already growing fond of each other. On the 9th of March, 1963, they observed an old Ford coupe traveling slowly, its license plate not illuminated, making an illegal U-turn. Officers Campbell and Hettinger pulled the car over. Campbell, the lead officer on the traffic stop, ordered the driver out of the car. As the driver, Gregory Ulas Powell exited, he pulled a gun on Officer Campbell and disarmed the officer. Karl Hettinger drew his gun and aimed it intermittently at the driver and the front-seat passenger. The driver ordered his cohort, Jimmy Lee Smith, to disarm Officer Hettinger. Hettinger would not give up his gun. Powell said that he would shoot Campbell if Hettinger did not put down his weapon. Hettinger held his ground until his partner told Hettinger to put his gun down. And so Hettinger gave up his gun, and so the nightmare began.

All four men crammed into the little Ford and Campbell was forced to drive, a gun at his side at all times, another gun trained on Hettinger in the back. All along the drive, the two officers were given every reason to believe that they would be released, in a very remote area, but unharmed. Campbell was directed to come to a stop in the middle of a deserted onion field. Powell told the officers that this is where they were going to be let go, to find their own way back to the highway. Both officers were, at this point, ordered out of the car. There they stood, together again, their arms raised high above their heads. Guns, their own guns and the suspects' guns were pointed straight at them. Powell walked around the car and reportedly said the following chilling words, "Well, we were going to let you go, but, have you ever heard of the Little Lindbergh Law?*" . Officer Campbell answered "yes". That answer earned him a bullet in the mouth. He was shot four more times in the chest after he was already down, dying in the middle of all those onions. Karl Hettinger screamed, turned, and ran. He ran and ran and ran, the murderers of his partner shooting at him, desperately trying to hunt him down all the while, in the middle of all those onions. Ian Campbell died that night, and his partner did not. Karl Francis Hettinger died on the 4th of May, 1994, but his spirit was unquestionably killed on the 9th of March, 1963.

Hettinger went right back to work after the kidnapping and murder and he was almost immediately bombarded with questions regarding the incident. His superiors made Hettinger speak at every roll-call and recount the events of that night to all of his fellow officers. A superior officer is said to have made the comment that any officer who gives up his weapon in the line of duty is a "coward". Instead of referring to the murderers of Ian Campbell as cowards, that is how Karl Hettinger was referred to, within his own police department. He suffered from insomnia and kleptomania after the incident and he visited multiple therapists. Within a short amount of time, Hettinger was a shell of his former self, mostly due to the insensitive way he was treated by his department. He was ordered to resign from the Los Angeles Police Department after he was caught shoplifting, even though Hettinger's kleptomania was diagnosed as "survivor's guilt", and an urge to be punished for failing to save Ian Campbell's life. Karl

---

*The "Little Lindbergh Law," passed after the kidnapping of the Lindbergh baby, mandated that kidnapping, for ransom with bodily harm only be counted as a capital crime, punishable by death. However, since Campbell and Hettinger were not being held for ransom, and had not been harmed at that point, the crimes committed by Powell and Smith that night only became capital crimes after Campbell was murdered.

Hettinger's stealing was not the act of a criminal, it was the act of a desperate, suffering man. Despite the neat, rather tidy ending found at the conclusion of the film-adaptation of Joseph Wambaugh's account of The Onion Field, Karl Hettinger never recovered from the events of the 9th of March, 1963, nor the abuse inflicted on him by the LAPD. Ian Campbell did not die because of the actions of Karl Hettinger, he died because of the actions of Gregory Powell and Jimmy Lee Smith.

It is nearly impossible for the police officer in America to get it right. Whatever he does, it is most certainly wrong. It truly is against the law to shoot and against the law to miss. The four NYPD officers shot, and it was wrong. Karl Hettinger didn't shoot, and that was wrong too. Until the job of the police officer is done by a robot, there will always be mistakes and, because the events that police officers deal with every day are of such a high-stakes nature, sometimes innocent blood will be spilt. No, that is not okay, but it is a reality of life. Police officers are not perfect, they are merely humans asked to go do a super-human job. It is my one and only hope that this book makes you think about those humans. Give them a second thought. Understand what they live for, and what they die for. Know that it is not just for a tin star, but it is for so much more— it is for you, and it is for me. They are but human beings, and when the bagpipes bleat out a mournful dirge for one of them, you should feel that shiver, racing up and down your spine, even if you are not physically there to hear it. Most of all, the next time you see a police officer sitting in his patrol car or strolling down the street, walk up to him, put out your hand, and say "thank you". Don't wait until he's lying in a satin box, surrounded by flowers and mourners, because then you'll never get to see him smile.

Funeral Orders

"The most sublime act is to set another before you."

— *William Blake*

Funeral Orders

Weep, thou square-shouldered men, thou hard-faced women,
The thousands of you here today shall cry together all,
On his shoulder or hers you shall rest your weary heads,
For, as wetness rains down from the Heavens, so too,
Shall it pour on from your sad and terrified blue eyes.

Salute, thou uniformed throng, thou soldiers of the law,
You must all pay respect today, you must honor the debt,
The widow is passing by now and for her you must be strong,
No harsh words shall be spoke, my friends, no weapons shall be drawn,
There are no killers now to wrestle with, now grieving takes its turn.

Play, thou minstrels of death, thou muses of cruel pain,
Your drums will coax this fallen one to his all-too-early grave,
Keep sharp now all your hands and play well this requiem,
Intone you now the pipes, I say. Cry on, hard notes, cry on!
Your skirling sounds may haunt some hearts, but heal all Law today.
Pray, thou earnest chaplain, thou wise and gracious priest,
Help these despondent masses to stand up and rise again,
To walk again their beats of filth, to work again their shifts,

Tell them they are righteous, give them comfort all today,
Share with them their anger as you share with them your Love.

Stand, thou wounded woman, thou innocent, wronged youth,
Be always brave and always proud, but let the mourners help,
For though, it's true, in hell you walk, don't face the flames alone,
Hold fast your friends' hands, for now they are your solace,
Widow, live amongst the living, not the void, black like your dress.

Wail, thou mechanized voices, thou screaming siren's song,
Bleat out your anguished yelps as the martyr's march prowls on,
Howl louder for this hero, bring good people from their homes,
Call them out to witness, let them all for certain know,
They have one less good protector, that the law has been assailed,

And so wail today, so wail.

Gabriel L. Nathan

Memorial to slain Philadelphia police officers. Gabriel Nathan, photographer.

ABOUT THE AUTHOR

Gabriel Nathan is currently an undergraduate at Muhlenberg College in Allentown, Pennsylvania where he is a theatre major with an acting concentration. He has been published in the OP/ED section of the *Philadelphia Daily News* once and the *Philadelphia Inquirer* four times. His commentary on the slaying of Philadelphia Police officer Daniel Faulkner, "Epiphany at Officer's Grave" originally appeared in the *Philadelphia Inquirer* on 23 January, 2000 and can be viewed on the internet at www.mumia.net. In addition, he writes short stories, one-act plays, and poetry. His poem, "A Patrolman's Departure" was published in the Philadelphia-area law enforcement magazine, *The Peace Officer.* The poem can also be viewed on numerous internet police memorial websites. Gabriel has been an active advocate for living and slain law enforcement officers for approximately six years.